Antique Cast Iron

Antique Cast Iron

Michael Owen

BLANDFORD PRESS

POOLE   DORSET

First published 1977
Copyright © 1977 Blandford Press Ltd.
Link House, West Street
Poole, Dorset BH15 1LL

ISBN o 7137 0833 6

Printed in Great Britain by Staples Printers Ltd.

Contents

Acknowledgements

I am indebted to a number of people and firms for their kindness, cooperation and help: notably the Kenrick family of Archibald Kenrick and Sons; Mr. William Brown of the Carron Company; Mr. Bushell and his staff of the Dale Works of the Allied Ironfounders; Mr. Neil Cossons, Director of the Ironbridge Gorge Museum Trust; I also thank them all for permitting me to use the illustrations from their catalogues and collections; to Mrs. B. Newport for reading the text before publication, and making valuable suggestions for its improvement.

Foreword

As the first industrial nation, Britain is rich in the remains of eighteenth- and nineteenth-century industrial activity. The Industrial Revolution was first and foremost a revolution in the techniques of making things, and so we tend to think of its effects on the landscape in terms of factories, mills and warehouses and their associated transport systems—canals and railways. But industrialisation had a far greater impact on our surroundings, not only in the great manufacturing centres which it created, but in every town and village in the country, in urban and rural areas alike.

New production methods afforded artists and designers creative opportunities which had never existed before; one particular process, the manufacture of iron castings, provided the foundation for a whole new industry, which had a radical effect on the appearance of places like Bath and Cheltenham. Iron casting lends itself ideally to the repetition of large numbers of identical objects and because each casting originates from a pattern, often carved in wood, it was exploited as a medium uniquely suited to the artistic, manufacturing and entrepreneurial enthusiasm of Georgian and Victorian England. The gentry and the new middle classes aspired to live in elegant towns where they could forget the ravages of industry upon the landscape; paradoxically, they also sought to surround themselves with the products of the industry most fundamental to the development of the Industrial Revolution.

Michael Owen recognises this and in relating the surviving hardware to the documentary evidence, and in particular to the catalogues of the major manufacturers, he establishes the credentials not only of railings, balconies or fireplaces but such everyday things as the door-knocker and the foot-scraper. Abraham Darby, who at Coalbrookdale in 1709 perfected the technique of smelting iron with coke instead of charcoal, is rightly regarded as a pioneer technologist of the early industrial age and the company which he founded led the way to the large scale use of cast iron by the mechanical and civil engineer. Michael Owen identifies in this book what is perhaps the most tangible and instantly recognisable memorial to the work of the Darbys of Coalbrookdale and the other great ironfounders, the decorative and architectural cast ironwork which adorns many of our finest towns and cities.

Neil Cossons
Director, Ironbridge
Gorge Museum Trust
Ironbridge, 1977

Preface

The recent upsurge of interest in Industrial Archaeology is
most gratifying, and has fortunately become part of serious
study just in time. Yet oddly enough, the study of domestic
items, particularly in cast' iron, has almost escaped notice.
This may have occurred because many of these items are still
sufficiently common not to have attracted much attention.
However, a time can be foreseen when this will no longer be
the case, if they continue to be ignored.

This book is an attempt to rectify this situation, and it takes
a closer look at domestic cast iron. Certain items are omitted
for reasons of space and the depth of understanding which is
required. These include flat irons, pots and pans, pokers,
shovels, tongs and kitchen ranges, where a knowledge of
heating engineering is necessary.

This study sprang from the collection which I am amassing
in the U.K. at the Roman Baths Museum in Bath. Items are
being collected from buildings due for demolition. A number
of illustrations come from this collection.

In other instances, when illustrating material from the old
catalogues, their pages have been reproduced here as facsimiles.
The period style of notation (not to mention the original prices)
contained in the catalogue pages adds considerably to the at-
traction of the articles and sets them firmly in context.

It would certainly be impossible to illustrate everything
ever produced and so readers and collectors may discover
styles not here illustrated. This does not mean that I did not
know of their existence, or that I ignored them, but is merely
that they represented a variation on a general type. A fully
comprehensive survey of all styles of hob grates earlier than

1820 would mean visiting every house earlier than that date, which would clearly be impossible.

Setting aside personal taste, which has no relevance to a study of this type, there is little doubt that the second half of the nineteenth century saw the most adventurous and best iron casting that there has ever been. This book is in many ways a tribute to the ingenuity and brilliance of the iron casters and, I hope, will encourage a greater interest in the subject. If it also means that more evades the scrap metal merchant, succeeding generations will thank us. We should not judge nor belittle the achievements of our ancestors, we should conserve them.

Michael Owen
Bath, 1977

Chapter 1

The Rise of Cast Iron

Until the beginning of the eighteenth century, the production of cast iron relied upon smelting with the use of charcoal. This resulted in cast iron works being sited within reach of both the iron ore and the forests which produced the wood for charcoal. In England, this accounts for iron works being sited, for instance, in the Weald area of Kent and Sussex.

The transformation in iron-smelting came at the beginning of the eighteenth century. A pioneer in this field was Abraham Darby senior, who moved his works from Bristol to Coalbrookdale, Shropshire, in 1709. Here, a charcoal furnace had been in existence since 1638, but Darby adapted it to smelt iron ore with coke. From this small beginning the British cast iron industry was to undergo a revolutionary change and experience expansion.

Coal, from which coke was produced, was slowly replacing charcoal for smelting, but the process was fairly slow as not all coal proved to be satisfactory when coked for use in smelting. Around 1750, production by the use of coking coal had already affected the charcoal production of iron.

From the middle of the century, development became more rapid, and the improved cast iron was influencing the inventors and engineers. This produced an accelerating spiral, for the more ideas and products that the inventors and engineers came up with, the more cast iron was needed, and the more quickly the industry expanded.

The steam engine was employed to produce the blast for the furnace, which produced a greater reduction of the ore, while coke was a better smelting agent. The old charcoal pig-iron was apt to 'run thick' but the coke-smelted iron was more manageable.

The inventors and engineers were also affecting matters in another direction. As a result of various inventions, discoveries and new civil engineering techniques, communications were improving. There were new roads, bridges and canals which made transport easier and less expensive. A dramatic result of this can be seen in the completion of the canal from Birmingham, via Smethwick and Bilston, to Wolverhampton in 1767. This brought about a reduction in the price of coal in Birmingham from 13s a ton to 8s 4d a ton (a reduction from 65p, or about $1.00, to 42p, or about 75c).

This easing of communications made it possible for both iron and coal to be transported to centres of production. Thus industry began to be concentrated in areas rather than be scattered. This resulted in greater efficiency and economy.

By the 1770s, many types of castings were being produced by these new and much larger iron works, and the first cast iron bridge in the world was produced in 1778. This bridge can still be seen at Coalbrookdale, Shropshire.

This was all very well, but how did it influence the domestic market, or the domestic market influence the cast iron industry? This part of the story falls into two categories, namely the social upheaval of the time, and the changing requirements of fuel.

The Renaissance in Europe brought many changes to the land, which were slowly absorbed during the sixteenth and seventeenth centuries. These two centuries saw many changes in the standard of living. An increasing proportion of the population enjoyed a higher standard of living, and the people in the higher social status commanded many servants.

One of the results of this was the break-up of the simple Mediaeval divisions of the home. The house structure became rather more complex, rooms became less lofty, and better insulated by the use of plaster on the ceilings and panelling on the walls. Central hearths had gone and even the very large hall fireplace backing onto the cross hall was disappearing. The result of a proliferation of rooms was the need for many fireplaces and hearths, with the corollary of many more flues and chimneys. The great size of chimneys was not so necessary, for not only would they overpower the rooms, but would also consume an enormous quantity of fuel. Thus, social demands were changing to meet a new set of circumstances.

Running parallel to this, however, the type of fuel used was also changing. It is fortunate that the extraction of coal in quantity came when it did. Otherwise, a very embarrassing situation might have occurred, where even noble and royal households were without heat.

The consumption of wood had continued apace throughout the middle ages, for so much relied upon its use; much building was done in wood, all ships were built of wood, wood was used on domestic fires, and by all smiths to make charcoal for smelting.

A few examples will perhaps show clearly the deterioration which took place because of the lack of any systematic policy of replanting in the British Isles. At Windsor Castle in 1354, accounts refer to over 3000 oaks being felled, and in 1361–1362 a further 2000. In the times of Charles I, the Forest of Dean was estimated to contain 105,000 trees; by the Restoration this figure had dwindled to 30,000. In 1635, a perambulation of Wolmer Forest had revealed that it had hardly any trees. Between the reigns of Elizabeth I and William III, the vast Forest of Arden, covering most of Warwickshire north west of the Avon, disappeared.

Coal appeared only just in time to save the situation. It was, of course, a very different commodity to burn from wood. Unlike large pieces of tree it did not require a huge fireplace in which to burn, and the 'Firedogs' or 'Andirons' as they are often called, became redundant. It was realised, however, that to burn at all efficiently, the fire would still need to be raised from the hearth. The immediate reaction was the basket grate placed within the fireplace, but as we know well today, the quantity of smoke within the room must have been enormous.

It is here, then, that the changing social patterns and the different requirements of a new fuel became united. The obvious answer was smaller fireplaces—and they certainly became smaller—but the nuisance of smoking chimneys did not dwindle. This curse must have been much less of a nuisance in the middle ages with the huge, lofty halls, than it was in the lower smaller rooms of later centuries. In such situations, it must have been a menace!

There then followed a whole range of attempted cures for smoking chimneys, which were nothing if not ingenious. There were such inventions as Prince Rupert's Fireplace of 1678, which one suspects he did not find too trustworthy, for he advises stoking little and often; and then there is Dalesme's Heating Machine, which had to be stoked upside down! But this and Prince Rupert's, like other inventions of the period, relied on cleverly arranged extraction pipes. Thus, they were difficult to start, for until these pipes were warm, they would not work properly. It is amusing to speculate on the frustrations and anger this must have caused in cold weather!

Other methods were devised, and all were attempting to channel the smoke away, or at least greatly restrict the opening through which the smoke would travel and thus concentrating the draught in one spot. Still much of the problem came from the distance between the grate and the chimney opening. An attempt to eliminate this problem resulted in the Taphouse grate and the Bathgrate being tried. The Bathgrate seems to have been a great favourite in the later eighteenth century.

However, fire grates are not the only domestic areas in which cast iron was of value. For when considering door knockers, balconies, and railings, then another interchange of ideas is again evident.

The eighteenth century saw a great concentration of population within towns and the growth of all classes of society living within them. Houses evolved accordingly. The increasing number of callers at front doors resulted in some form of knocker, rather than the callers injuring their knuckles rapping on hard wood.

Urban communities produced open spaces in the form of squares, parks, courts, and terraced houses with little land for gardens. Balconies outside windows, to hold flower boxes, or on which to stand tubs, became popular features.

The development of urban houses had produced two further features: taller houses, and kitchens housed in basements or semi-basements, which necessitated an area being provided outside the basement kitchens in front of the house, for light and air; thus a fence from the pavement or road to prevent people and traffic falling into the void, became an essential, and railings formed this fence.

As the potential of cast iron became more fully appreciated, the variety of objects produced in this material increased. Not only were door knockers produced, but fine door knobs for internal and external use were also manufactured.

Letter boxes followed the introduction of the penny post in 1840 and a considerable variety of styles ensued.

The quality of roads still left much to be desired, so foot scrapers became a useful, if not necessitous piece of equipment.

Inside the house, door porters, or door stops became most useful, as anyone with rising hinges and strong draughts will appreciate.

The fireplace was beautified; ash was not a very nice sight in the grate, so ash guards were designed, fenders delineated the fireplace, and trivets provided places where kettles could be placed.

So confident did the manufacturers become, that not only did styles proliferate but banisters, newel posts, and even complete staircases were produced in intricate designs.

Wright, L. *Home Fires Burning* Routledge and Kegan Paul, 1964

Chapter 2
Balconies and Railings

The previous chapter has set out the reasons for the appearance of the various articles to be described in the remainder of the book.

In an attempt to create a logical sequence, the description commences from the exterior and proceeds to the interior of the house. Balconies and railings are, thus, the first to be considered.

Balconies

Perhaps one of the most difficult things to decide is how many of these are of cast iron and how many of wrought iron. Figure 1 shows that large portions of a balcony were cast, but how much of the smaller parts were similarly cast? Figures 2 and 3 show that cast or wrought railings could be added to cast heads. Thus, appearance alone can sometimes be deceptive. There is, however, a further consideration to which thought must be given.

A vast quantity of building was taking place from the middle of the eighteenth century onwards and to which a great quantity of railings and a large number of balconies were being attached. Is it reasonable to expect that the wrought iron craft kept pace with an ever accelerating demand? Was it not better for the customer and producer alike, to have cast examples where production-rate would be higher and delays in deliveries much less? Then as now, delay undoubtedly caused frustration and resentment.

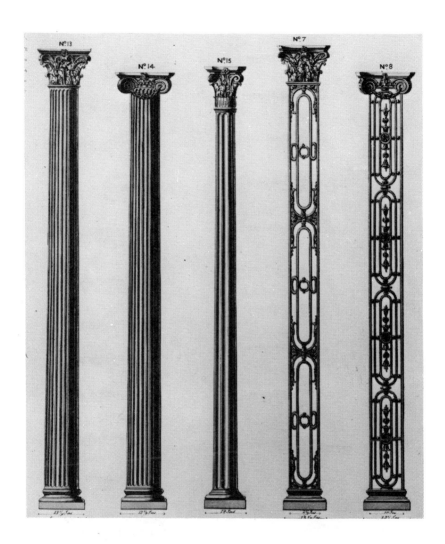

Fig. 1   Verandah members from Coalbrookdale catalogues. On the left are three columns, with two verandah pilasters on the right.

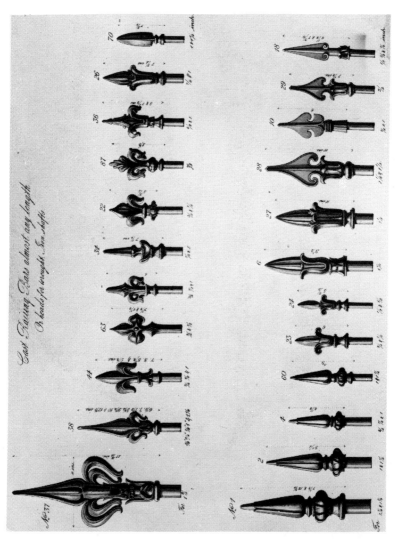

Fig. 2   Railing beads from the Coalbrookdale catalogues.

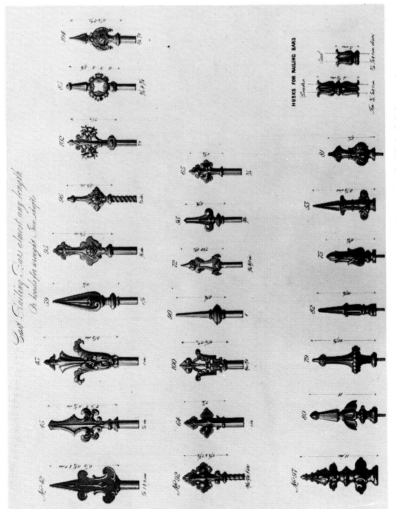

Fig. 3 Railing beads and basks (bottom left) *from the Coalbrookdale catalogues.*

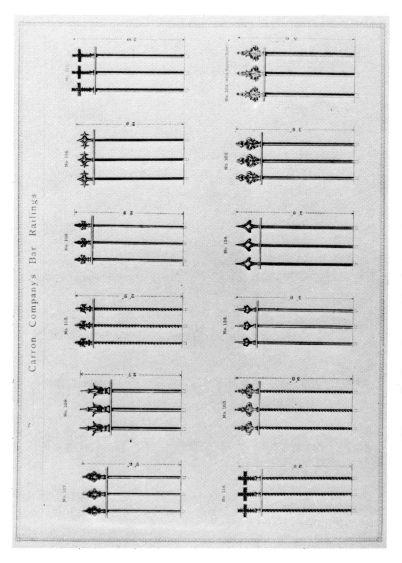

Fig. 4   Railings, bars and beads, from the Carron catalogues.

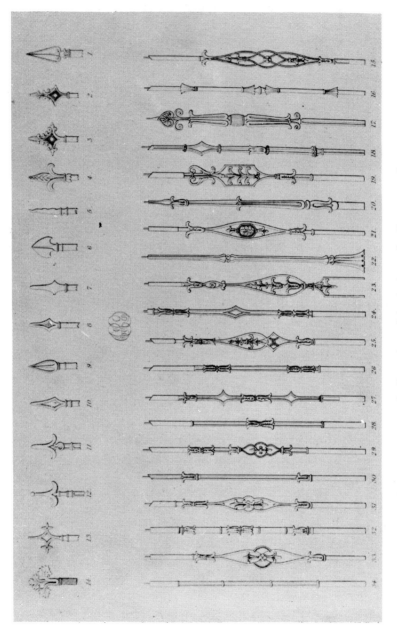

Fig. 5 Railings (ballasters) and beads from the Carron catalogues.

I suggest, therefore, that much more of this material is made of cast iron than might at first be suspected. While there is an element of doubt here, there is a need for an examination rather than for a brush to sweep the subject under the carpet.

The distinction between cast and wrought iron can best be illustrated by two small balconies in Fig. 6. The lower is a wrought iron example of flat, hammered parts. This is very evident from the uneven, roughly circular shapes at the base, and to a lesser extent from the pointed arch arrangement at the top. The sub-circular shapes at the base are constructed of two roughly semi-circular pieces joined together.

While it is folly to try to date optional extras on buildings (such as balconies and door knockers) from the date of the building, it would not be surprising if this example, was not added soon after its erection in 1770, at a stage when cast iron for domestic items was only just gaining momentum.

The upper part of Fig. 6 illustrates an entirely regular and delicate balcony in a diagonal cross pattern with the top rails parted by small spheres. The spheres are perfectly regular, the base of the circular cross section are certainly cast and it is probable that the other members are also cast. It is quite possible to produce a cast, as well as wrought iron flat bar.

Another interesting feature seen here is the number of rosettes located where the diagonal bars meet. These are made of lead and must have added considerably to the overall effect when originally produced. It is a pity that they are generally smothered in paint these days.

This balcony cannot be earlier in date than 1793 when the building was completed. It is probable that this balcony dates from just after 1800.

The other problem is the way the items were assembled. The manner in which wrought iron was constructed is obvious enough, but in cast examples it is far less apparent. These were seemingly assembled in much the same manner as wrought iron, the lead rosettes being used to cover the joins and to add decoration where dullness might otherwise result.

Fig. 6 Three balcony styles for single windows.

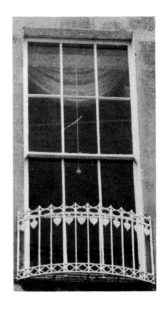

Fig. 7 Balconies on larger verandahs, open and covered.

Fig. 8   Balcony Styles.

Fig. 9   Balcony Styles.

Fig. 10   Balcony Styles.

Fig. 11   Balcony style for semi-circular balconies.

At this stage, where all the individual pieces (however small) were assembled on erection, there was a comparatively limited range of ideas which could be followed or which appealed at the time. The delicacy achieved by these was not attained again; artistic fashion was to ensure this. Good examples of this delicate work can be seen in Fig. 7 which was probably erected when built in 1808 or very soon after, Fig. 8, Fig. 9 and Fig. 10—these latter two showing signs of more elaborate panels, but not at this stage cast as one piece.

The next stage in the development was the casting of complete panels, the beginnings of which can be seen by the Greek key pattern of Fig. 8 and Fig. 10, where it is also probable that the imitation trellice work was similarly treated. The example shown in Fig. 13 shows lengths of balcony railing which show beyond doubt that sections were cast in units. The sections were arranged in the decorative order required and fitted into the available space. The sections were held rigidly in place by joining, at intervals, to top and bottom rails.

The development then continued further and the same motifs are endlessly repeated. Figure 11 where the outward curve at the bottom of the lower picture would have provided casting problems, Fig. 9 and the alternating designs of Fig. 10 and Fig. 12 show an elaborate repeated pattern the date of which is 1830 or some years later.

The above covers balconies of two types. Firstly, small single window balconies, which even with a plank would barely have carried a person and would have been of little use had they so done. Their use was most likely for carrying flower-boxes and this is often the purpose to which they are put today.

Secondly, we have considered the large double or treble window balconies large enough to carry persons and pot plants. To use these one supposes the individual waited for dry and hot weather and then staggered out with chairs to sit in state and survey the view and the world at large! The openness of these cannot have been everything to be desired, so the wealthy or prudent added a canopy over the top, Fig. 7, and in some cases canvasses were used to cover the sides. Both these additions made a balcony more useful and less of a white elephant which merely required maintenance.

The other items of which no mention has yet been made is the lamp bracket. These might be mounted on a single cast balcony detail like Fig. 1, or fixed rather splendidly over the pathway. This could be done in a modest manner like Fig. 14 or more handsomely as in Fig. 14. This latter example was produced by joining cast strips and cast panels. The only way, however, to produce a lamp-holder must have been by cast strips or wrought pieces as Fig. 14 clearly shows.

Railings

Little has yet been said anywhere about railings, of which thousands of miles must have been made and the vast majority, I am quite sure, were cast. It is very doubtful whether many, except the rather eccentric, would bother to purchase a set

Fig. 12 Balcony styles.

Fig. 13   Balcony railing designs from the Carron catalogues.

Fig. 14 (a)   An integrated design of archway, lampholder and railings.

of cast ornamental tops and then have them laboriously attached to wrought iron bars. Perhaps the only people who might are those of the older generation who were suspicious of the new ideas, and come what may, preferred traditional methods.

The types of tops illustrated in Figs 2–5 cover quite a range of time and these are offered as tops for wrought bars; but I suspect the manufacturers were gently amused by such a

Fig. 14 (b)   A simpler style of lampholder, incorporated with railings.

laborious request. Figure 14 shows a fine set of railings, undoubtedly all cast, as indicated by the urn shape appearing regularly in the lengths.

Although the evidence is not available, it would be interesting to have comparative prices of wrought and cast items where both methods of manufacture were possible. It seems a reasonable conjecture that casting, which was a method of uniform mass-production, was considerably cheaper than the laborious hammerings of wrought iron. With the improvement of technique, when whole sections were cast together, the cost would fall even further, for less time would be spent in producing a greater quantity.

Did the idea of balconies cross the Atlantic to the United States? It is reasonable to expect, correctly, that it would—but obviously British styles did not. The evidence readily available shows that American styles differ markedly from their British counterparts. Both cast and wrought iron types exist, but it is obvious that the distinction between cast and wrought is not appreciated. In the book *Early American Wrought Iron* (Plates 230 and 234) both items from New Orleans, are both cast and not wrought.

Taste in decorative style in the U.S.A. was, like its colonising population, extremely varied. Taste was thus an amalgam of ideas from varying backgrounds. British taste only appealed to a proportion of the population. To import or copy on this basis was probably a risky procedure—particularly where optional items were concerned.

Chapter 3
Door Furniture

Knockers

The most impressive door furniture is certainly the large variety of door-knockers which can be seen on many doors of the Georgian and Victorian styles of houses.

The need for knockers has already been explained in Chapter 1. It must have been prior to the end of the eighteenth century that door-knockers appeared, for the firm of Archibald Kenrick and Sons, the most important producers, was founded in 1791.

It is fairly certain that competition in Britain was not excessive for Kenrick in the first half of the nineteenth century, as undoubted Kenrick knockers possess no stamp on the back displaying the firm's name. From then on, Kenrick products seem generally to be stamped, which may reflect the increase in producers.

These new producers, in spite of the registering of designs, were most likely copying designs, for the same types occur in the catalogues of a number of makers. The Dale company produced some knockers, but this was not their main line of production. It is probable that Dale made them as customers might be persuaded to buy them while they were purchasing grates.

Other producers were comparatively small and included Tipper Bros. and W. P. Edmunds. From the evidence to be found in catalogues, these smaller firms succeeded by running popular lines at a price which considerably undercut those of

Kenrick. Prices of the same styles from the Kenrick 1840 catalogue are higher than those of Edmunds of some time later.

Price is a fascinating subject. The earlier Kenrick catalogues show prices beside each article as can be seen from the illustrations. Prices ranged from a shilling (5p) to around three shillings (15p) each, which suggests that they were not all that cheap for the time. Kenrick in 1840 were offering No. 364 (Fig. 20) at the cheapest a shilling (5p) each. Edmonds price of some time later is ten shillings (50p) a dozen.*

There are only two ways in which it is possible to build up any chronological sequence of types. These are by appearances in catalogues and by styles.

It is a pity that Kenrick's catalogues do not exist prior to 1840, but luckily a substantial number of the types ever produced are illustrated from thence forward—although even by this date there are more than a few omissions, probably as a result of deletion and succession. Any attempt to date knockers by the date of the building on which they hang is doomed to failure. Knockers are portable and can be moved from house to house with an owner, or can be discarded in favour of a more recent design.

In retrospect, there seems to be three main phases of new productions. The late eighteenth and early nineteenth centuries, from 1830, and from 1870. The styles of the three main phases are mirrors of taste, although, at first one expects that styles lagged behind trends in design. This was probably because door-knockers were produced as much for existing doors as for doors on new buildings. Knockers for existing buildings required classical designs, such as urns, lion's heads, annulets and similar styles. It was not until markets had become reasonably steady that design became bolder and fashionable. When it was discovered that these bolder, fashionable designs were appreciated and purchased, designers let their imaginations run wild. The result was many of the later bold and highly ornate designs.

*Spring 1977, $=£1·72

Nº 114 ____ 1/3 ea
Nº 114 A
Brass name plate } 1/9

Nº 116 __ 1/2

117 _ 1/1
118 _ 1/3
119 _ 1/6

Nº 120 ____ 1/1
Nº 121 ____ 1/4
Nº 122 ____ 1/8

Nº 123   1/2

Nº 126 A ____ 1/1
Nº 126 ____ 1/2
Nº 127 ____ 1/4
Nº 128 ____ 1/8
Nº 129 ____ 2/-

Nº 261 __ 1/9

Nº 306 _ 2/3

Nº 307 _ 1/3

Nº 311 _ 1/2

Nº 310 ____ 1/2
Nº 310 A ____ 1/4
Nº 316 ____ 1/8

Nº 304 _ 2/3

Figs 15–30   Doorknockers from the Kenrick catalogues.

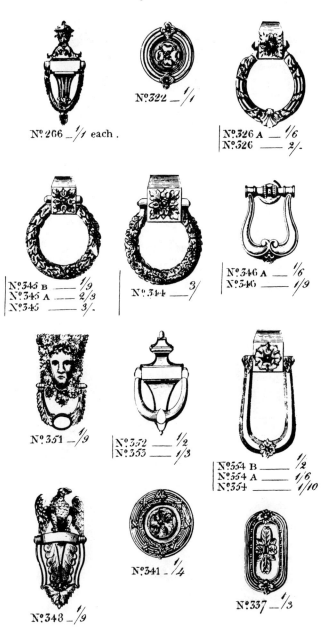

Nº 266 — 1/1 each.

Nº 322 — 1/1

Nº 326 A — 1/6
Nº 326 — 2/-

Nº 345 B — 1/9
Nº 345 A — 2/3
Nº 345 — 3/-

Nº 344 — 3/

Nº 346 A — 1/6
Nº 346 — 1/9

Nº 351 — 1/9

Nº 352 — 1/2
Nº 353 — 1/3

Nº 354 B — 1/2
Nº 354 A — 1/6
Nº 354 — 1/10

Nº 348 — 1/9

Nº 341 — 1/4

Nº 337 — 1/3

Fig. 16

Nº558 . 1/2 each

WELLINGTON

000 1/6 | 0 2/6
00 2/- | 1 3/-

Nº540 3/-

Nº524 B 1/1
Nº524 1/3
Nº525 1/5

Nº545 1/3

Nº277 1/2

Nº549 1/6

Nº282 1/4

Nº550 1/4

Nº555 2/9

Nº556 2/9

Nº559 1/3
559A 1/9

Fig. 17

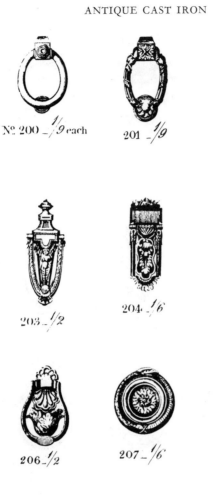

No. 200 _ 1/9 each   201 _ 1/9   202 _ 1/6

203 _ 1/2   204 _ 1/6   205 _ 1/3

206 _ 1/2   207 _ 1/6   208 _ 1/1

209 _ 1/2   210 _ 1/3   211 _ 1/2

Fig. 18

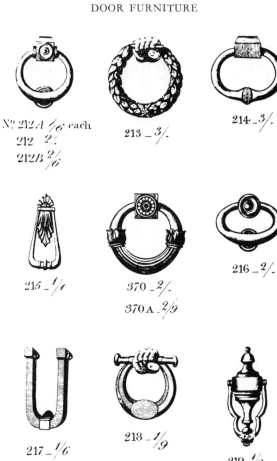

Nº 212A 1/6 each
212 2/.
212B 2/6

213 _ 3/.

214 _ 3/.

215 _ 1/1

370 _ 2/.
370A 2/9

216 _ 2/.

217 _ 1/6

218 _ 1/9

219 _ 1/2

220 _ 1/6

221 _ 1/6

222A _ 1/3
222 _ 1/6

Fig. 19

355 A
2/3_ea.

356 A
2/6

357
2/-

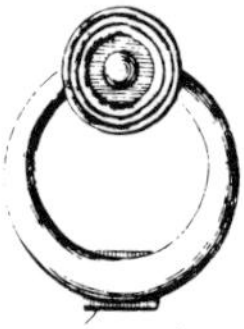

Nº568A _ 1/6
„ 568B _ 1/9
„ 568 _ 2/-

365
_____ 1/9
Brass Center _ 5/6
365 B _ 1/3
365 A _ 1/6

363
1/6

364
     s d
_____ 1_3
Brass Center 3_6
364x 1_0

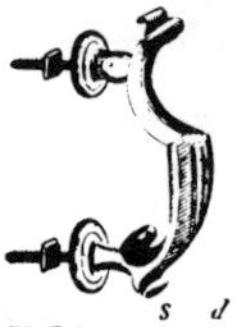

Nº359 s d
      2 0
„ 360 2 3
„ 361 2 6

369
 s d.
2.0

223
1/6

371- 1s.6d.

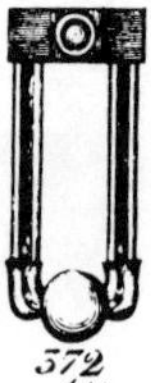

372
1/8

Fig. 20

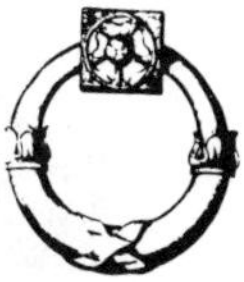

Nº 373 _ 2/. each.

374 _ 1/6

375 _ 2/.

376 _ 1/6

377 _ 2/

380 _ 1/4

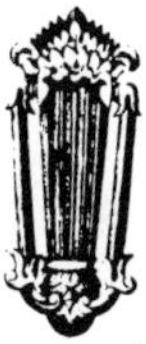

379 B _ 1/1
379 A _ 1/2
379 _ 1/4

378 _ 2/6

381 _ 1/3

382 _ 1/4

383 _ 1/9

384 _ 1/9

Fig. 21

Nº 385 — 1/4 each.

387 — 2/6

386 — 1/6

8 In Diamʳ

388 — 1/9

389 — 5/6

390 — 1/6

391 — 1/2

392 — 1/9

395 — 1/7

394 — 1/10

395 — 3/.

396 — 2.

Fig. 22

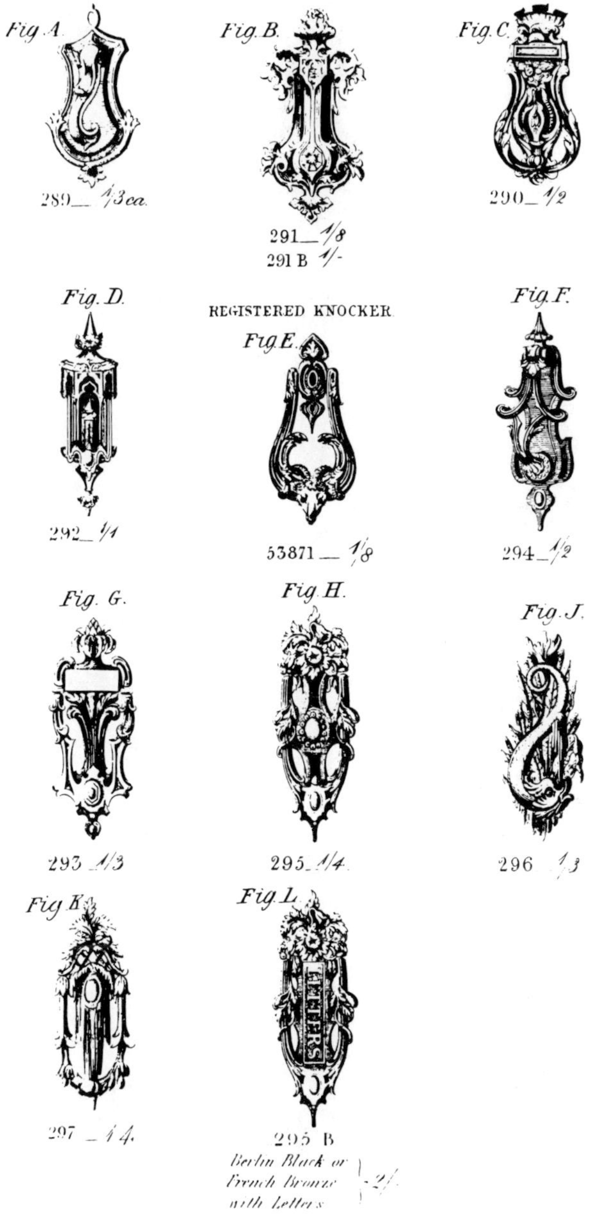
Fig. A.
289 — 1/3 ca.
Fig. B.
291 — 1/8
291 B 1/-
Fig. C.
290 — 1/2
Fig. D.
292 — 1/1
REGISTERED KNOCKER
Fig. E.
53871 — 1/8
Fig. F.
294 — 1/2
Fig. G.
293 — 1/3
Fig. H.
295 — 1/4
Fig. J.
296 1/3
Fig. K.
297 — 1/4
Fig. L.
LETTERS
295 B
Berlin Black or French Bronze with Letters — 2/-

Fig. 23

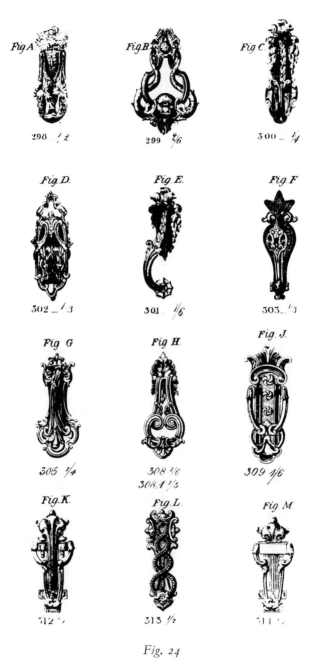

Fig A
298 _ 1/2

Fig B
299 2/6

Fig C
300 _ 1/4

Fig. D.
302 _ 1/3

Fig. E.
301 . 1/6

Fig. F
303 _ 1/3

Fig G
305 1/4

Fig H.
308 2/6
308.1 1/3

Fig. J.
309 1/6

Fig. K.
312 1/2

Fig. L.
313 1/2

Fig M
311 1/2

Fig. 24

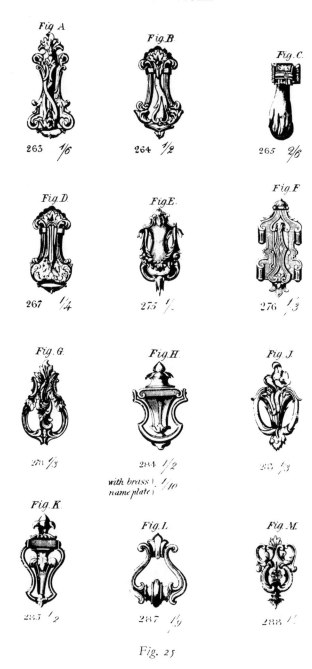

Fig. 25

37

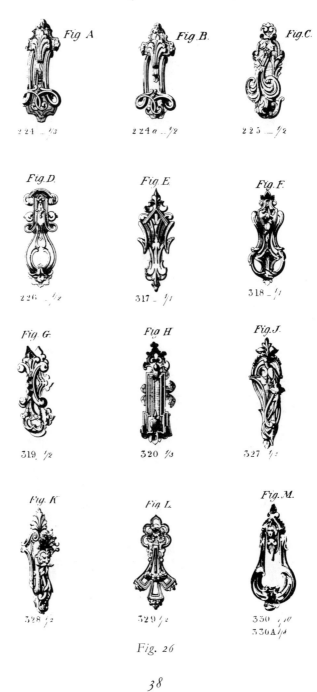

Fig. 26

38

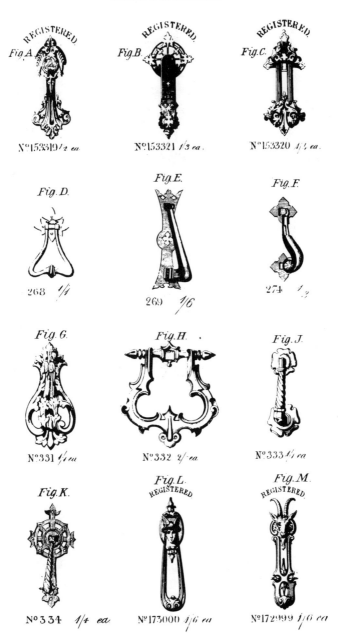

Fig. 27

Fig. A.
REGISTERED

№ 209636 /4 ea

Fig. B.
REGISTERED

№ 209633 /4 ea

Fig. C.
REGISTERED

№ 209634 /4 ea

Fig. D.
REGISTERED

№ 209635 /4 ea

Fig. E.
REGISTERED

№ 209632 /6 ea

Fig. F.
REGISTERED

№ 209637 /4 ea

Fig. G.

№ 1304 1/6 ea

Fig. H.

№ 1467 1/4 ea.

Fig. 28

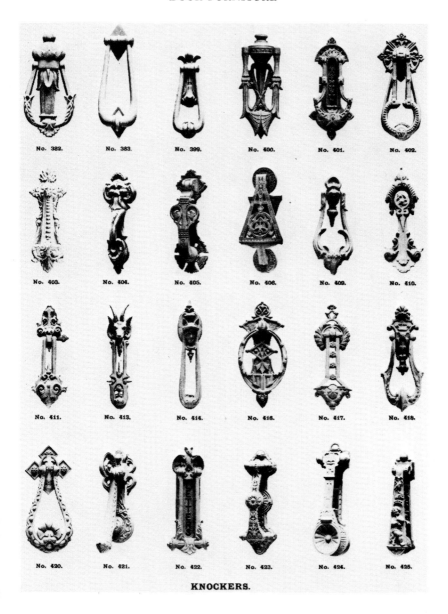

No. 382. No. 383. No. 399. No. 400. No. 401. No. 402.

No. 403. No. 404. No. 405. No. 406. No. 409. No. 410.

No. 411. No. 413. No. 414. No. 416. No. 417. No. 418.

No. 420. No. 421. No. 422. No. 423. No. 424. No. 425.

KNOCKERS.

Fig. 29

Relative occurrence of Door Knockers in the Catalogues of Archibald Kenrick and Sons, Ltd.

Pattern	1840	1871	1880	1899	1926
Wellington	*	*	*		
114	*	*	*		
116	*	*	*		
117/119	*				
120/122	*				
123	*	*			
126/129	*	*	*		
200	*				
201	*				
202	*				
203	*	*	*	*	
204	*	*			
205	*	*	*	*	
206	*	*	*		
207	*				
208	*	*			
209	*	*	*	*	
210	*	*			
211	*				
212	*				
213	*	*			
214	*				
215	*	*	*	*	*
216	*				
217	*				
218	*	*			
219	*	*			
220	*	*			
221	*	*			
222	*	*	*		
223	*				
224		*	*	*	
225		*	*	*	*
226		*	*		
227		*			
228		*			
229		*	*	*	
274	*	*	*	*	
275		*			
276		*			
277	*	*	*	*	*
278		*			
282	*	*			
283		*			
284		*			

Pattern	1840	1871	1880	1899	1926
285		*			
287		*			
288		*			
289		*			
290		*			
291		*	*	*	
292		*	*	*	
293		*	*	*	
294		*	*	*	*
295		*	*	*	
295B		*	*	*	*
296		*	*		
297		*			
298		*			
299		*	*		
300		*			
301		*			
302		*			
303		*			
304	*	*			
305		*	*	*	*
306	*				
307	*				
308		*	*	*	
309		*	*	*	
310 & 316	*	*	*	*	
311		*	*	*	
312		*	*	*	
313		*	*		
314		*	*	*	
317		*	*		
318		*	*		
319		*	*		
320		*	*		
322	*				
324/5	*	*	*		
326	*	*			
327		*			
328		*	*		
329		*			
330		*			
331		*			
332		*	*		
333		*	*	*	
334		*	*		

Pattern	1840	1871	1880	1899	1926
337	*	*			
338	*	*			
339	*	*	*		
340	*	*			
341	*				
343	*	*	*		
344	*				
345	*				
346	*				
348	*	*	*		
349	*	*	*		
350	*	*			
351	*				
352/3	*				
355	*	*	*		
355A	*				
356	*	*			
356A	*				
357	*				
359/61	*	*			
363	*	*			
364	*	*	*	*	*
365	*	*	*	*	*
368	*				
369	*	*			
370	*	*	*		
371	*	*			
372	*	*			
373	*	*	*		
374	*	*	*		
375	*				
376	*	*			
377	*	*	*		
378	*	*			
379	*				
380	*				
381	*	*			
382	*	*	*	*	
383	*	*	*	*	
384	*				
385	*				
386	*				
387	*	*			
388	*				
389	*				
390	*	*	*		
391	*	*			
392	*				
393	*				

Pattern	1840	1871	1880	1899	1926
394	*				
395	*	*			
396	*				
397	*				
398	*	*			
399	*	*	*	*	*
400			*	*	
401			*	*	*
402			*	*	*
403			*		
404			*		
405			*	*	*
406			*		
407(1304)		*	*		
408(1467)		*	*		
409(53871)		*	*	*	
410(153319)		*	*	*	
411(153320)		*	*	*	
412(153321)		*	*		
413(172999)		*	*	*	
414(173000)		*	*	*	*
415(209632)		*	*		
416(209633)		*	*	*	
417(209634)		*	*	*	
418(209635)		*	*	*	
419(209636)		*	*		
420(209637)		*	*	*	
421			*	*	
422			*	*	*
423			*	*	*
424			*	*	*
425			*	*	*
426			*		
427			*	*	
428			*	*	
429			*	*	
430			*	*	
431			*	*	
432			*		
433			*	*	
434			*	*	
435			*	*	
436			*	*	
439		*	*	*	
440		*	*	*	
441			*		
442				*	*
443				*	*

No. 427. No. 428. No. 429. No. 430. No. 431. No. 433.

No. 434. No. 435. No. 436. No. 439. No. 440. No. 441.

No. 442. No. 443. No. 444. No. 445. No. 446. No. 447.

No. 448. No. 449. No. 450. No. 451. No. 452. No. 265.

KNOCKERS.

Fig. 30

The early phase of production is of designs which have classical, symmetrical and reasonably restrained subjects. Typical are classical faces, circles or ovals, variations on the urn and animals such as the lion and eagle accompanied by foliage or flowers, normally grapes or roses. Of these undoubted early designs, it is fascinating to see that Nos. 364–365 (Fig. 20) and No. 277 (Fig. 17) are still to be found in the 1926 catalogue. It is interesting to see how much can be made from the circle and oval, from the hand clasping a ring, to a horseshoe like a drop piece. Many of the types illustrated in Figs 15–17 belong to this early production but amongst these are the beginnings of the next major group from 1830.

The group from 1830 are probably represented by types 206, 209, and 391, but these are far more obvious in the collection in Figs 22 and 23. This group has a completely different feeling from those of the previous period. Here are far more florid, fussy designs, but ones which were keeping abreast of trends and fashions. When one thinks of the amount of building in the Victorian era this was likely to have produced a massive sale.

Many of these designs are both good and clever. The interlaced designs whether plain geometric or serpents, the grotesque faces and animal heads are all very fascinating.

In the 1840 catalogue are illustrated what must be the latest designs, these with 'Registered' above them and the long number Figs 23 and 27.

The third major group from 1870 contains a further collection, the designs of which are an extension of the previous trend (Figs 29 and 30). The elephant trunk No. 452 and the cherub No. 425, which still appears in the 1926 catalogue, are fine examples.

Letter-boxes

Amongst the collection of knockers will have been noticed a few letter-boxes or letter-plates as they are known. Quite a large group of letter-plates were produced after the intro-

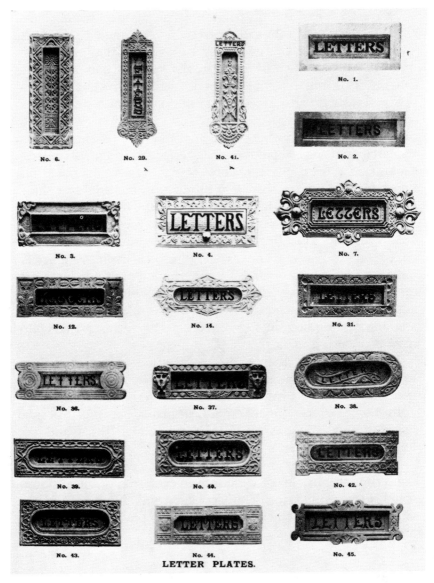

No. 6. No. 29. No. 41. No. 1.

No. 2.

No. 3. No. 4. No. 7.

No. 12. No. 14. No. 31.

No. 36. No. 37. No. 38.

No. 39. No. 40. No. 42.

No. 43. No. 44. No. 45.

LETTER PLATES.

Fig. 31   Letter plates from the Kenrick catalogues.

46

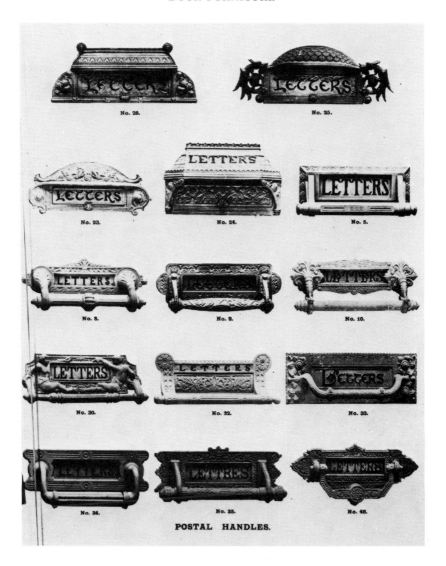

Fig. 32   Letter plates, showing incorporated handles, from the Kenrick catalogues.

47

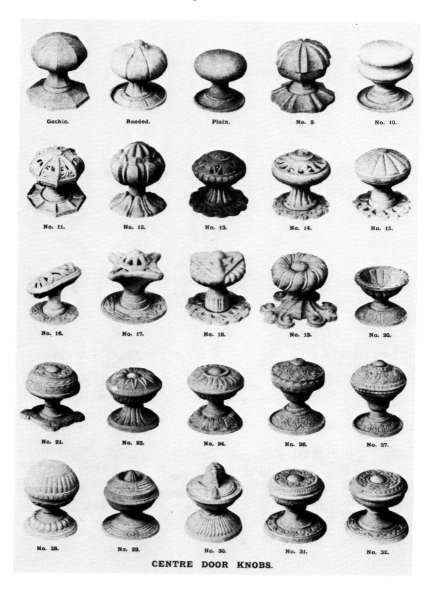

Gothic.   Reeded.   Plain.   No. 9.   No. 10.

No. 11.   No. 12.   No. 13.   No. 14.   No. 15.

No. 16.   No. 17.   No. 18.   No. 19.   No. 20.

No. 21.   No. 23.   No. 24.   No. 26.   No. 27.

No. 28.   No. 29.   No. 30.   No. 31.   No. 32.

CENTRE DOOR KNOBS.

Fig. 33   Centre door knobs from the Kenrick catalogues.

duction of the British penny post in 1840. No. 295B (Fig. 23) is an interesting immediate reaction, while the two alongside it are obviously prepared in a hurry. Having taken a breath and given some thought to the subject, quite a quantity of types gradually appeared and this can be seen by the fine group from the 1880 catalogue. Some have handles and have quite exotic designs like Nos. 25 and 30 (plate 32). A very popular line was the combined knocker and letter-plate surmounted by a bat: No. 422 (Fig. 29).

Knobs

Lastly, in the survey of door furniture are the large centre knobs which gained popularity in the second half of the nineteenth century. This popularity may be due to people no longer wishing to swing on knockers to close doors—or to have their fingers caught in the letter-plate as the spring on the back automatically closes on them! It is scarcely credible that so much can originate from such a simple thing as a door knob; imagination is very considerable and ingenious (Fig. 33).

Dating the items

It is impossible to provide the year of production for many examples, but for a period a registration system was listed for articles of metal, wood, glass and ceramics.

From 1842 until 1883, all objects in these materials carried a registration mark in the form of a diamond surmounted by a disc. The disc carried the class number. The classes were I metal, II wood, III glass and IV ceramics. Until 1868, the letter immediately beneath the disc gave the year of manufacture, the month in the space at the left hand side of the diamond. The number on the right hand side gave the day of the month, and that at the bottom indicated the manufacturer. From after 1868 and until 1883, the number positions were altered. The class number remained the same, but the year letter went to the right hand side, the month letter at the

Code for Dates of Manufacture of Domestic Cast Iron 1842–1883

MONTHS

C	January	E	May	D	September
G	February	M	June	B	October
W	March	I	July	K	November
H	April	R	August	A	December

YEARS

X	1842	L	1856	C	1870
H	1843	K	1857	A	1871
C	1844	B	1858	I	1872
A	1845	M	1859	F	1873
I	1846	Z	1860	U	1874
F	1847	R	1861	S	1875
U	1848	O	1862	V	1876
S	1849	G	1863	P	1877
V	1850	N	1864	D	1878
P	1851	W	1865	Y	1879
D	1852	Q	1866	J	1880
Y	1853	T	1867	E	1881
J	1854	X	1868	L	1882
E	1855	H	1869	K	1883

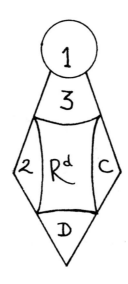

The registration mark used to date articles.

bottom, the day number at the top beneath the disc and the manufacturer number to the left-hand side (see opposite).

For some reason, after 1883, the system was discontinued. It may be that so much material of all four classes was by then being produced, that the system was unworkable, or that for some time manufacturers had been evading the system.

Any system such as this provides the date for a specific example, but fails to provide information on the first appearance of a type. The only source of this is the first appearance in a catalogue where succeeding years' catalogues exist. If no catalogues exist, then guesswork is the only method, and this is not very reliable. Without a 'national door knocker census' it would be impossible to give accurate figures on the relative prevalance of earlier or later types; but in my experience from Bath, a city of many buildings which pre-date door knockers, later types constitute approximately seventy per cent of the types collected. However, this is reasonable, for not only would new buildings be provided with modern styles, unless a disreputable builder bought a consignment of superseded stock at a bargain price, but also moneyed people tended to replace older styles of knocker by the latest model.

Most door furniture will still be found on doors of houses of appropriate dates, although more are now appearing in the more avant-garde type of antique shop.

The firms producing the material have a lack of examples of their own products. To my knowledge the collection which I am amassing in the U.K. at Bath is, if not the only, one of very few existing collections.

Chapter 4
Scrapers and Door-porters

Before finally going within the house, scrapers and door-porters need to be considered.

Although roads and sanitation were improving in the nineteenth century, they still left much to be desired. Roads and pavements were no doubt very dirty with mud, rubbish and other less desirable material. The necessity for scrapers, to at least remove the main bulk of the rubbish carried on the feet was virtually essential, to prevent the undesirable from being tramped on to polished floors and carpets.

Door-porters, as will be apparent are door stops. The problem of rising hinges and wind is one which can be solved in no other way.

Scrapers

There are three types of scrapers: those to be fixed to the wall, those to be fixed into stone, and a portable variety with an attached pan to collect the dirt.

It is quite easy to see why there were few varieties of wall scrapers, for the majority were impractical. The shoe would catch on the wall, thus scratching the leather, while at best a poor cleaning would be achieved.

In contrast, scrapers set in stone were clearly a very much better arrangement for a fixed style. They could be used by the whole foot and did not fall over or damage the shoe.

Pan scrapers were a general purpose variety, being portable and therefore had uses within or without the house.

Exactly when scrapers were introduced cannot be ascertained, but types 405, 416, 417, 420, 421, 423, 424, 490, 491, 494 and 495 certainly belong to a stage of design probably prior to 1830 (Fig. 34). As can be seen from the examples illustrated here and which are in the 1840 catalogue, plenty existed by this time.

This 1840 catalogue shows that the same influences were affecting the designs of both scraper and door knockers. Animals, birds and foliage were important design features. More noticeable here, however, is the influence of the Gothic on designs of this date; Nos. 574, 579 and 584 are particularly good examples of this style (Figs. 35, 37 and 38).

A number of designs are reminiscent of railway tunnel entrances, noticeably Nos. 481, 483, 485 and 486 (Fig. 34). It will be observed that some designs appear both as pan scrapers and those set in stone (Nos. 519 and 600, 574 and 603, and 404 and 413).

The new examples in the 1871 catalogue (Fig. 42) show a continuing interest in railway architecture, but a subtle change of emphasis has occurred. The feeling of Nos. 620, 621, 623 and 624 has a touch of the Egyptian, whilst Nos. 623 and 624 provide an uncanny reminder of the Clifton Suspension Bridge at Bristol.

When reviewing the survival rate, it has to be remembered that by 1900 roads had much improved and from then on were to be affected by the requirements of the motor-car, and its offspring, in the form of lorries and vans carrying increasingly heavy loads. Very few fixed scrapers survive in the 1926 catalogue, but more of the portable pan type remain, although fewer than might be expected. Conditions in Britain were altering by this time, but one would not expect scrapers to have become obsolete. Britain was entering the age of the semi-detached suburban house, back gardens, and plenty of mud caused by the normally over-wet soil—a consequence of the climate. Perhaps the apparent demise is, however, the result of good sales publicity on behalf of the manufacturers of coconut mats!

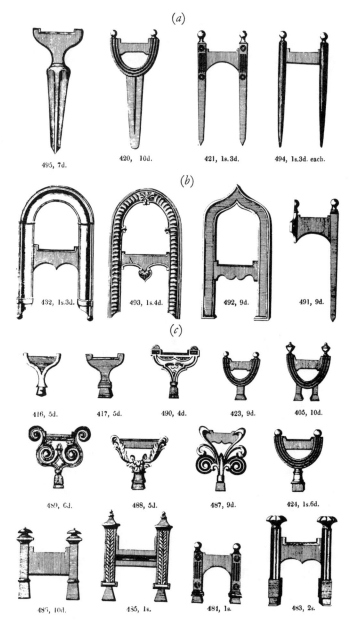

(a)

495, 7d.   420, 10d.   421, 1s.3d.   494, 1s.3d. each.

(b)

432, 1s.3d.   493, 1s.4d.   492, 9d.   491, 9d.

(c)

416, 5d.   417, 5d.   490, 4d.   423, 9d.   405, 10d.

489, 6d.   488, 5d.   487, 9d.   424, 1s.6d.

486, 10d.   485, 1s.   481, 1s.   483, 2s.

Fig. 34   *Scrapers from the Kenrick catalogues;* (a) *Garden Scrapers,* (b) *Wall Scrapers,* (c) *Scrapers to set in stone.*

560 _ /6 ea.   561 _/9   562 1/-   563 _/5

564. 1/-   565 1/8   566 1/8   567 _/-

568 _ 1/2   .569 _/-   570 _ 2/3   571 1/3
Wrought tongue.

572 /9   573 /10   574 1/-   575 1/4
Wrought tongue

576 1/8   .577 1/9   579 2/-
French pattern   Wrought tongue

Figs 35–38   *Scrapers to set in stone, from the Kenrick catalogues.*

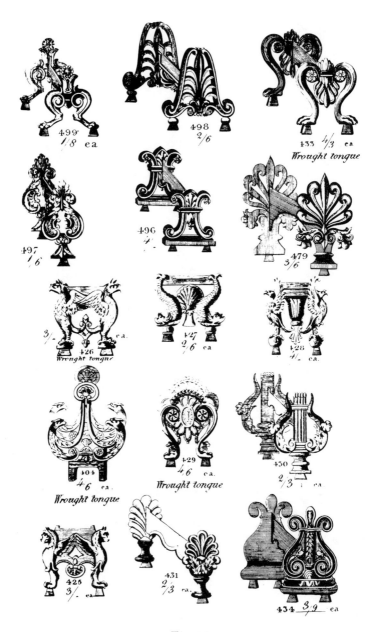

Fig. 36

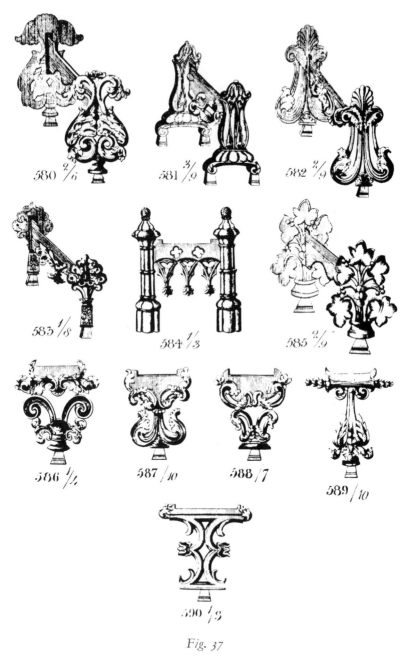

Fig. 37

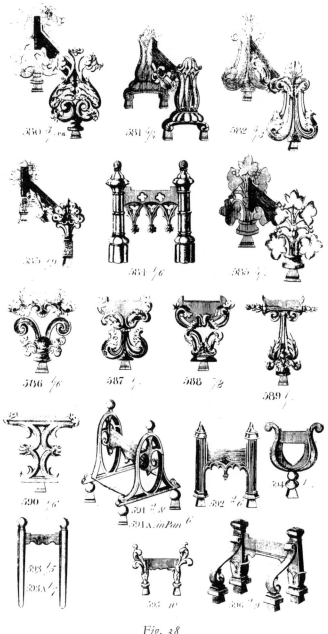

Fig. 38

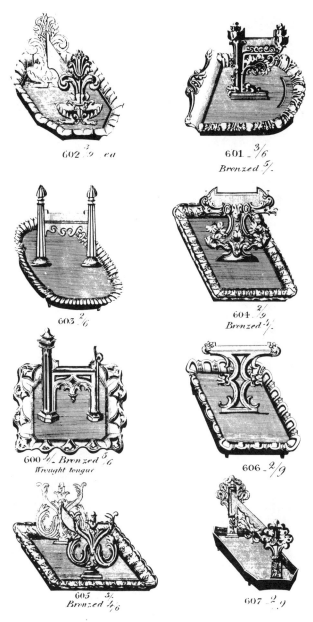

Fig. 39   Pan scrapers from the Kenrick catalogues.

608 *4/. each.* 609 _ *3/9*

610 _ *2/-* 615 _ *5/9*

Fig. 40   Pan scrapers from the Kenrick catalogues,

613 *With Brushes.____*
Without Brushes. ____

614 *With Brushes.*
Without Brushes.

Fig. 41   Kenrick pan scrapers incorporating cleaning brushes.

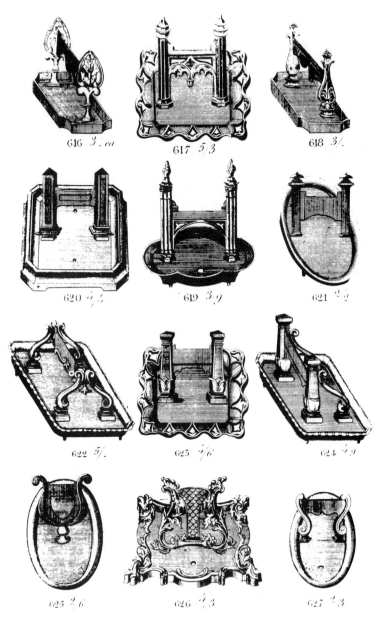

Fig. 42   Pan scrapers from the Kenrick catalogues.

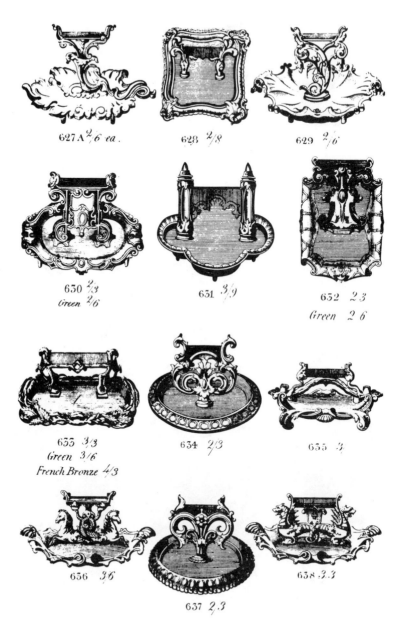

627A 2/6 ea.   628 2/8   629 2/6

630 2/3
Green 2/6

631 3/9

632 2 3
Green 2 6

633 3/3
Green 3/6
French Bronze 4/3

634 2/3

635 3

636 36

637 2,3

638 3.3

Fig. 43 Pan scrapers from the Kenrick catalogues.

62

Occurrence of Scrapers in the Catalogues of
Archibald Kenrick and Sons Ltd.

SCRAPERS

Pattern	1840	1871	1880	1899	1926
404	*	*			
405	*	*			
416	*	*			
417	*	*			
420	*	*	*	*	
421	*	*	*	*	
423	*	*			
424	*	*			
425	*	*			
426	*	*			
427	*	*			
428	*	*			
429	*	*			
430	*	*			
431	*	*	*		
432	*	*	*		
433	*	*			
434	*	*			
479	*	*			
483	*	*			
484	*	*			
485	*	*			
486	*	*	*	*	*
487	*	*	*		
488	*	*	*		
489	*	*	*		
490	*	*	*		
491	*	*	*	*	
492	*	*	*	*	
493	*	*	*		
494	*	*	*		
495	*	*	*	*	
496	*	*			
497	*	*			
498	*	*	*	*	
499	*	*			
560	*	*			
561	*	*	*	*	*
562	*	*			
563	*	*			
564	*	*			
565	*	*			
566	*	*			
567	*	*			

SCRAPERS

Pattern	1840	1871	1880	1899	1926
568	*	*			
569	*	*			
570	*	*			
571	*	*			
572	*	*			
573	*	*	*		
574	*	*	*		
575	*	*			
576	*	*			
577	*	*	*	*	
579	*	*			
580	*	*			
581	*	*			
582	*	*			
583	*	*			
584	*	*	*	*	
585	*	*			
586	*	*			
587	*	*			
588	*	*			
589	*	*			
590	*	*			
591		*			
592		*			
593		*	*		
594		*			
596		*	*	*	
597		*	*	*	*
598		*			
599		*			
650		*			
651		*			
652		*			
653		*			
654		*			
655		*			
656		*	*		
661/2			*		
666			*	*	
671			*	*	
672			*	*	
674			*	*	*
686				*	

Occurrence of Scrapers in the Catalogues of
Archibald Kenrick and Sons Ltd. (cont.)

PAN SCRAPERS

Pattern	1840	1871	1880	1899	1926
400	*	*	*	*	*
401	*	*	*		
402	*	*	*		
403	*	*	*	*	*
406	*	*			
407	*	*	*	*	*
408	*	*			
409	*	*			
410	*	*			
411	*	*	*	*	
412	*	*	*	*	*
413	*	*			
414	*	*	*	*	
415	*	*	*		
418	*	*	*	*	
419	*	*	*	*	*
422	*	*	*	*	
435	*	*			
436	*	*			
437	*	*			
438	*	*	*	*	
439	*	*	*	*	
480	*	*	*	*	
481	*	*	*	*	
482	*	*	*		
500	*	*	*		
501	*	*	*	*	
502	*	*	*	*	
600	*	*			
601	*	*			
602	*	*	*	*	
603	*	*	*	*	*
604	*	*	*	*	
605	*	*			
606	*	*	*		
607	*	*			
608	*	*			
609	*	*	*		
610	*	*	*		
611	*	*	*	*	
612	*	*	*	*	
613	*	*	*	*	*

PAN SCRAPERS

Pattern	1840	1871	1880	1899	1926
614	*	*	*	*	*
615		*			
616		*	*		
617		*	*		
618		*	*		
619		*	*	*	
620		*	*		
621		*	*	*	*
622		*			
623		*	*		
624		*			
625		*	*	*	
626		*	*		
627		*	*		
627A		*			
628		*	*	*	
629		*			
630		*	*		
631		*	*		
632		*			
633		*	*	*	
634		*	*		
635		*			
636		*	*		
637		*	*	*	
638		*	*	*	
639		*	*	*	
640		*	*	*	
641		*	*	*	
642		*	*	*	
643		*	*	*	
644		*	*	*	
645		*	*	*	*
646		*	*	*	
647			*	*	
658			*	*	*
659			*	*	
660			*	*	*
677			*	*	*
678			*	*	
684		*	*		
685				*	*

Door-porters

While the other producers did not specialise in the production of scrapers, again the smaller firms produced a few lines, but door-porters were produced in reasonable quantity by the Coalbrookdale Company as well as by Kenrick. This is amply exemplified by the illustrations from one of their catalogues.

A certain amount of design copying is evident, but who copied whom is not clear.

The types illustrated by both catalogues show a considerable variety and range of designs with human and animal figures. Definite features are Dale's seated 'Lion and Dog', and Kenrick's 'Highland Warrior'. These are notable examples, Some designs are like miniature fountains, for example Dale's No. 22, 23, 29 and 32; others are reminiscent of candle-sticks, bells and massive imitations of fobs. The use of foliage in many of these shows the popularity of its appeal at that time.

The designs of these many and diverse articles, while being typical of the period, show little allegiance to the Pre-Raphaelites—except in the case of the human figures, where serene, rather expressionless subjects are noticeable. This unreal approach to the human, unlike the splendid, lively, Mediaeval figures, is typical of the time.

The very busy nature of Victorian art, which many despise, seems to work very well in cast iron. This is, perhaps, because the design is not the only aspect to catch the imagination. It is also the quality of the casting which thrills and tempers the feelings which might otherwise mock the artistic ability.

The designers of these items are unknown. Francis Darby at Dale, however, during the later 1830s and 1840s, used some of the best British designers and imported others from France. Some of these items may be by Frenchmen or English-men such as John Bell, the designer of the great fountain 'Boy and Swan'.

It is worthy of note that the production of such items, and indeed all domestic casting, would need to be lucrative; for the number of designers, model makers, and associated staff

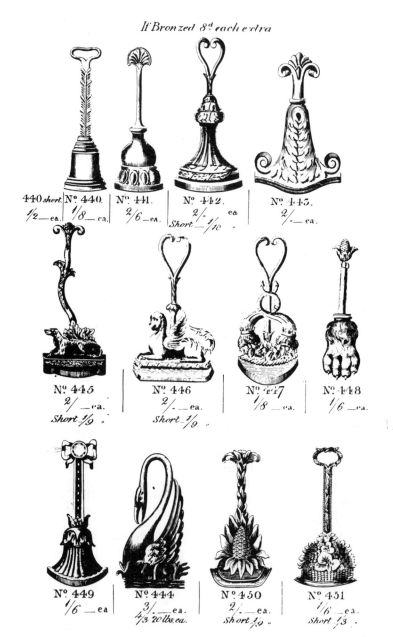

If Bronzed 8ᵈ each extra

440 short.

Nº 440.
½ — ea. ⅛ — ea.

Nº 441.
2/6 — ea.

Nº 442.
2/- ea
Short — 1/10 "

Nº 443.
2/- ea.

Nº 445
2/- ea.
Short 1/9

Nº 446
2/- ea.
Short 1/9 "

Nº 447
1/8 — ea.

Nº 448
1/6 — ea.

Nº 449
1/6 — ea

Nº 444
3/- ea.
4/3 20 lbs. ea.

Nº 450
2/- ea.
short 1/9 "

Nº 451
1/6 — ea.
short 1/3 "

Figs 44–47 Door-porters from the Kenrick catalogues:

If Bronzed 8 d. ea. extra.

452 _ 2/9 ea   453 _ 1/8   454 _ 2/_   455 _ 2/6
                                            Short 2/3

456 _ 1/9   457 _ 2/9   458 _ 2/9   459 _ 2/_
              Short 2/6   Short 2/6   Short 1/9

462
Short 1/2

460 2/_   461 _ 2/_   463 1/_   464 2/_
Short 1/9   Short 1/9   Short   Short 1/9

Fig. 45

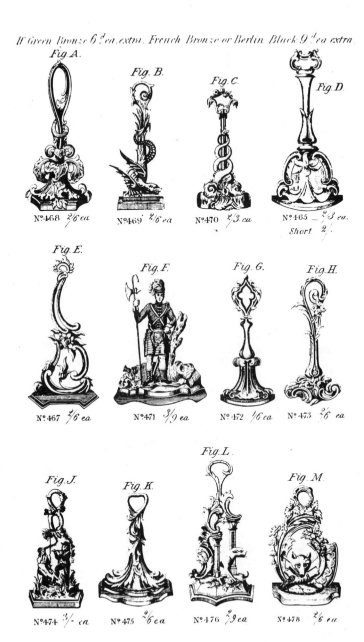

If Green Bronze 6ᵈ ea. extra, French Bronze or Berlin Black 9ᵈ ea extra.

Fig. A.

Fig. B.

Fig. C.

Fig. D.

Nº 468   2/6 ea

Nº 469   2/6 ea

Nº 470   2/3 ea

Nº 465 — 2/3 ea.
Short   2/-

Fig. E.

Fig. F.

Fig. G.

Fig. H.

Nº 467   2/6 ea

Nº 471   3/9 ea

Nº 472   1/6 ea

Nº 473   2/6 ea

Fig. J.

Fig. K.

Fig. L.

Fig. M

Nº 474   3/- ea

Nº 475   2/6 ea

Nº 476   3/9 ea

Nº 478   2/6 ea

Fig. 46

68

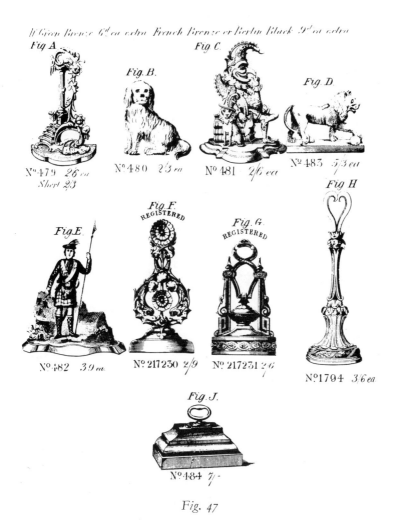

Fig. 47

would be considerable. The Dale Company in the middle of the nineteenth century employed some 3–4000 men and boys at Coalbrookdale and Horsehay. The entire output was 2000 tons a week and the works were the largest in the world. It is to be supposed that Kenrick's were no less successful although their works were smaller.

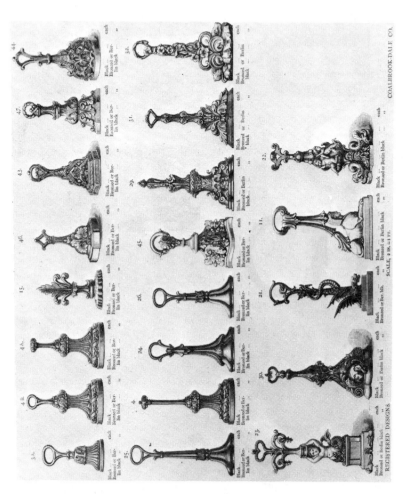

Fig. 48   Door-porters from the Coalbrookdale catalogues.

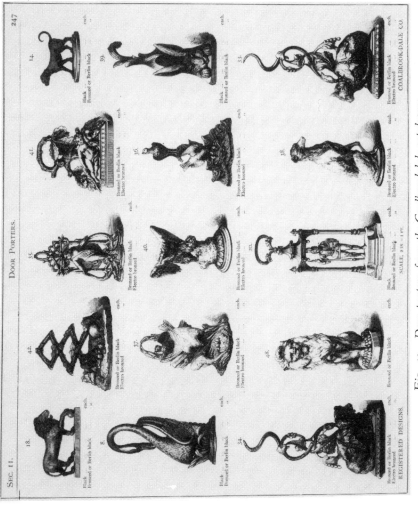

Fig. 49   Door-porters from the Coalbrookdale catalogues.

Occurrence of Door-porters in the Catalogues of
Archibald Kenrick and Sons Ltd.

Pattern	1840	1871	1880	1899	1926	Pattern	1840	1871	1880	1899	1926
440	*	*	*	*		465	*	*			
441	*	*				466		*	*	*	*
442	*	*				467		*			
443	*	*				468		*			
444	*	*				469		*	*		
445	*	*				470		*	*		
446	*	*				471		*	*		
447	*	*				472		*	*	*	*
448	*	*				473		*			
449	*	*	*	*		474		*	*		
450	*	*				475		*	*		
451	*	*				476		*			
452	*	*				477		*			
453	*	*	*	*		478		*	*		
454	*	*	*	*	*	479		*			
455	*	*	*	*		480		*			
456	*	*				481		*	*		
457	*	*				482		*	*		
458	*	*	*	*		483		*	*	*	
459	*	*	*	*	*	484		*	*	*	
460	*	*	*			485			*	*	
461	*	*	*	*		486(217230)		*	*		
462	*	*	*	*	*	487(217231)		*	*	*	
463	*	*	*			488			*	*	*
464	*	*				489				*	*

Chapter 5
Fireplaces

The fireplace, for centuries the focal point of the living room of any house, however great or small, is now being harshly treated with the advent of electric and gas fires and central heating. Fireplaces are sometimes entirely omitted in modern houses, a fact which would horrify our ancestors.

Happily this chapter is concerned with events prior to this dismal situation. In Chapter 1, enough has already been said about the changes occurring in living conditions and the arrangement of the house.

Control of draught and the proliferation of rooms requiring fires created the impetus for mass production of grates in which to burn the recently discovered coal. In an attempt to concentrate the draught, the basket grate was built into the fireplace, leaving fire bars only at the front. The back and sides were firstly made of fire bricks, then, later, a combination of fire bricks and cast iron, or cast iron alone. At first, the side pieces were of fire brick or stone, but their appearance was neither very decorative nor enhancing.

The result of this was the invention of the hob grate, which provided decorated front panels connected by a decorated piece. This not only held the panels together, but also the fire bars. In addition, the tops on either side made up the hobs on which kettles or saucepans simmered. The production of hob grates would have been impossible had it not been for the improved casting techniques pioneered during the first part of the eighteenth century. Two firms are the major producers. These are the Dale Company of Coalbrookdale and the Carron Company of Falkirk, Scotland, founded in 1759. At the onset, the most prominent firm in this field was the Carron Company, which was fortunate indeed to have Robert and James Adam as directors. These two were the initial impetus for many fine designs and were followed by William and Henry Haworth, both equally skilled and artistic. It is often asserted that the Dale Company was more concerned at this time with casting for heavy engineering and massive structures such as bridges. This is disputable for the greatest majority of grates in the collection at Bath dating up to 1830 are of Dale not Carron production. This certainly does not suggest a monopoly of the market for the Carron Company, or lack of competition on the part of Dale.

In following the various styles in grates, it is necessary to keep two ideas in mind. Changing fashions in art affect the design of the artistic part, while improved technology of heating or casting, or both, will promote changes in other features. The artist was undoubtedly sometimes kept very busy re-orientating to the latest technological improvements. One can do little but sympathise with the designer who has some really splended new styles up his sleeve, only to discover that the scientific revolution has made them of little, or even, no use.

The effect of the Adam brothers on the quality of design can be gauged by the work produced by them and by William and Henry Haworth. A problem arises in trying to differentiate between the work of these highly talented people. While, undoubtedly, the splendid urn in Fig. 52 is the work of the Adam brothers, equally, the battle trophies of Fig. 67 are the work of the Haworth brothers. The crossed trumpets with a ribbon to be seen on one of these presupposes that the cherubs within roundels in Figs. 63, 65, where the same motif occurs, are also the work of the Haworth brothers. The designs with pedestals and urns accompanied by foliage Fig. 50 and 51 probably are the work of the Adam brothers. This, however, is nearly as far as it is possible to take reasonably definite suggestions. The restrained oval and swags could be a Haworth design from the ribbon bow. It may well be that the classical figures surmounted on the cornucopia (Fig. 61) also are the work of the Adam brothers and that they then produced the work in Fig. 60—although it was probably by the Haworths. Following from this, the geometric designs of Figs. 55–58 are also Howarth work. For the fully geometric pattern, an intelligent guess suggests that again the Haworths were the designers.

Figs 50–67   Carron panels for fire grates.

Fig. 52   Fig. 53

Fig. 54

Fig. 55

Fig. 56

Fig. 57

Fig. 58

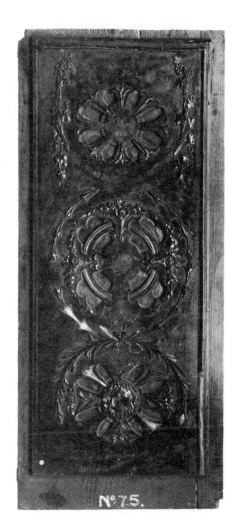

Fig. 59

Fig. 60

Fig. 61

Fig. 62   Fig. 63

Fig. 64   *Fig. 65*

Fig. 66

Fig. 67

Fig. 68(a)   Fire grates from the Carron catalogues.

Fig 68(b)   Two more fire grates from the Carron catalogue.

All the above examples are from patterns which fortunately still exist at Carron, but these are undoubtedly a very small proportion of the whole output. For instance, of all the Carron designs which I have discovered in Bath, only two are ones which I have seen at Carron. The remainder I had never seen and only knew the origin from the stamp on the particular item. It would certainly be anyone's guess who were the designers of those illustrated in Fig. 74.

So far, only the work of the Carron Company has been mentioned, Dale being almost entirely neglected. Alas, Dale patterns do not survive, but my own findings in Bath so far have produced many more Dale than Carron grates. I find no other reason, other than geography for this. It was probably considerably cheaper and quicker to transport from Shropshire than from Scotland. Probably you transported from Scotland if you could afford the time, the money, or both; or conceivably had an utter anathema to all Dale designs, but loved those of Carron. The latter idea is, perhaps, rather feeble. Although Dale had no Adam or Haworth, their designs followed fashion; indeed, sales would have been small if they failed to do so.

Certainly Dale designs were less ambitious than Carron's, but the urns and classical figures do exist (Fig. 70). The crossed trumpet and ribbon designs appear, but with different articles (Fig. 69) which is not the only example of design borrowing which can be found. Generally, at this stage, Dale shows less original genius; surely Fig. 71 is rather ordinary although pleasant. It would be hard indeed, to match the flair of the Haworths and the Adams.

The influence of Carron's geometric patterns upon Dale is quite clear. The likeness of Dale's geometric panel (Fig. 76) has an uncanny similarity to that of Carron's (Fig. 58). Geometrically arranged ideas seem to have been quite a speciality of Dale, particularly those, which on closer inspection, have unusual visual effects (Figs. 79 and 80). A further variation upon the geometric, but which includes designs within larger squares or rectangles, can be seen in Fig. 77. They seem to have a considerable relationship with some Carron types. An amusing side-line is from the Dale designer who may have been thinking nostalgically of home, depicting thistles on his panel. There is quite a range of Carron designs on the lines illustrated in Figs. 74 and 75. While the mutations cannot be infinite, they must be considerable. Some types are anonymous, which is rather tedious. Those shown on Figs. 69 and 70 are two such examples for which the only answer is the unreliable guessing game.

So far the examination has been of artistic styles prior to 1830; but also of relevance are casting methods and the shapes of the cast pieces. What appear to be the earliest grates are cast in the simplest manner. The earliest type would seem to be those with the complete front cast as one single piece, with only the fire-bars, hobs and internal strengtheners added. Examples of this stage are shown in Figs. 70–72, with the characteristically hemispherical upper and lower openings. While this arrangement had the advantage of simpler casting, it also had the disadvantage that the width was predetermined. It was impossible to alter the width when a fireplace was found to be of the wrong size. The only solution was to attempt to chop pieces from both sides. The result being more or less successful, and which I have seen more than once.

The logical development was to cast the side panels as separate units and join the two as a rigid whole, with a cross bar and the fire-bars. At first, an attempt was made to retain the hemispherical openings—as can be seen in Figs. 69–72. Finally, the panel became a rectangle and the cross piece became larger and, hence, a surface which could be decorated. The importance of this was clear; it mattered little what size was the fireplace, for by varying the size of cross piece and bars, many different sizes could be constructed.

The implication of this is clear. The various parts of the grates were cast separately and were then fitted together on site rather in the manner of so many kits of today. This was undoubtedly a very necessary arrangement for the space used on a wagon to convey a completed grate would be enormous, and thus make transporting costs, astronomical.

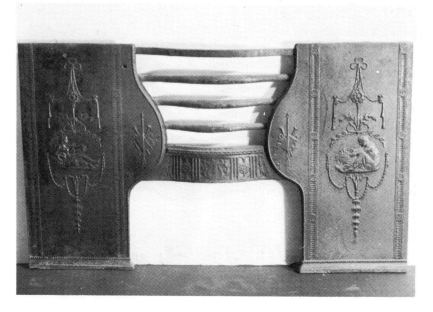

Fig. 69   Fire grates—upper *Dale;* lower *unknown.*

Fig. 70   Fire grates—upper *unknown;* lower *Dale.*

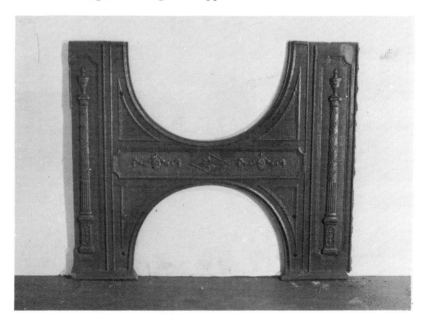

Fig. 71   Fire gates—upper *Dale;* lower *unknown.*

Fig. 72   Fire grates—upper *unknown;* lower *Dale.*

Fig. 73   Upper *Carron and Dale fire grate panels;* lower *unknown fire grate.*

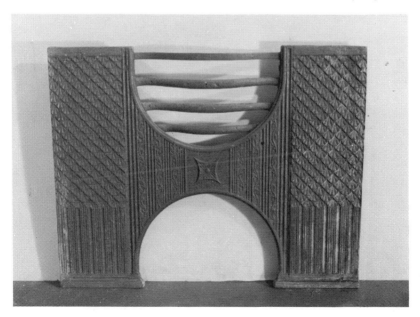

Fig. 74   Carron fire grates.

Fig. 75   Carron fire grates.

Fig. 76   Dale fire grates.

Fig. 77   Dale fire grates.

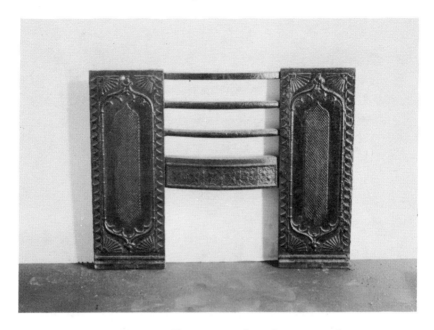

Fig. 78   Fire grates and panels—source unknown.

Fig. 79   Dale fire grates.

Fig. 80   Dale fire grate panel (above) *and Carron grate* (below).

Fig. 81 Top *Dale fire grate;* Lower left *Dale panel;* Lower right *Carron panel.*

Thus, a sequence has been built suggesting a logical development; but a sequence does not provide actual dates. To specify dates the only satisfactory and reasonably reliable method is by combining stylists tendencies, casting methods and occurrence within buildings, the dates of which are accurately known.

The geometrically styled grates all came from buildings dating 1815–1830, and this gives a rough guide at least. The sequence is from 1770, to 1800 for the original types; 1790–1815 for the intermediate stage; 1810–1830 or a little later for the rectangular panels.

The change in designs came about somewhere a little either side of 1830, a little before being the most likely. While the grate type remains the same, a considerable shift in design takes place. It is typified by the Dale grate shown in Fig. 81 and those in Fig. 82. It is uncertain in what direction designs were going. Some exhibit an aridity of idea which is frightening; although 2 and 2A at the bottom of Fig. 82 seem to be crystallising into a more familiar early Victorian design.

At this point, it is necessary to say a little more about fires and their performance. The hob grates burnt coal at quite a rapid rate, because draught control was almost non-existent. The only method of containing it at all would be by keeping a quantity of ash and clinker within the grate.

Smoke was undoubtedly still a frightful problem. A favourite way of solving the problem was the Bathgrate; so called it is believed, after its popularity in the city of Bath. This was simply the use of a semi-circular piece of metal inserted within the chimney opening, and attached to it, rather like a hood. This reduced the size of the opening and the distance from the fire to the chimney, and thus increased the draught and pulled the smoke upward. The modern use of copper canopies over open grates which is favoured in modernised houses and elsewhere is of the same principle. The popularity of Bath Grates was considerable. The following extract from the estimate in the original deeds for completing and finishing the Grosvenor Gardens and Hotel at Bath, designed and built by

John Everleigh in 1791, is of interest. For the sake of both interest and understanding, two paragraphs are included.

'The Hotel consists of four rooms on the Parlour floor; one very large and two smaller rooms on the Drawing room floor, five attics, six garretts with large and convenient underground offices, cellars, etc.

The whole to be roofed in; a stone staircase; the rooms on the Parlour floor to be finished with proper cornices, painted stucco, the two large parlours with marble chimney pieces, the others with plain Painswick stone. The rooms on the Drawing room floor with cornices, to be papered, and hansome marble chimney pieces; the Attics to be papered, Bath Stove Grates for all the rooms.'

Incidently, the cost was £1750.

A further development must be mentioned. This is the use of a cast iron back which can be seen in Fig. 7. The back was slotted into grooves of the side pieces. At first it was embellished little, but gradually ornamentation was added. By the early 1830s much decorative use was being made of these backs. This development is one to be noted, for it is a forerunner of what is to follow.

Apart from these fairly minor alterations, improvements seems to have been lacking between 1770 and 1830. How much of the developments after this was the responsibility of improvements in casting techniques, or renewed thinking on behalf of the heating experts is a matter for conjecture. From 1840 developments appeared which produce a radical change in the shape of the grate. Undoubtedly, the iron founders relished the increased quantity of cast iron being used in the new types, which drastically reduced the quantity of fire bricks. While improvements may have been made in some ways, there was probably a reduction in heat output. Cast iron is black and thus absorbs heat rather than reflecting it, and thus heat loss was probably inevitable.

Between 1835 and 1840 there occurred radical changes in designs. It is possible that the producers wished to make even greater use of cast iron by using more in grates. There was also a desire to scrap the rather clumsy Bathgrate hood, which was rather a problem to install. The best way to achieve this, was by casting the hood with the rest of the grate. This was basically a very good idea, but in an attempt to fill the whole fireplace, the hood was either abandoned altogether or raised so high that it was useless. Some of the examples and Fig. 87 and 84 show this very effectively. The problem was, if anything, further accentuated by the lowering of the grate and leaving it nearer the ground. This was not the most advantageous of ideas, except for the output of cast iron. The illustrations show that the whole grate is now in cast iron which includes backs, sides, and tops. These large castings continue with many variations thoughout the remainder of the century. Although the entire item was now cast, the various components were still joined together by nuts and bolts.

It is the designs, however, which are the most fascinating. The designers employed by Dale were certainly a rejuvenating influence. Figure 83 shows how reluctant were designers to part with the idea of the hob. The styles in Fig. 83 also show a new, refreshing approach; the ingenious use of curves, particularly in the upper three, is very striking and not unattractive. Foliage and floral designs are prominent. The bottom examples and Fig. 84 show the effective use of Gothic and Tudor Revival styles. There is a lack of unanimity on where to place the upper arch, and Nos. 66 and 27 are far too open. It seems to be a case where practicality is abandoned so long as the design is right. All depended on whether the individual wished a particular form of elegance, while suddenly being frozen and choked with smoke.

Nevertheless, one interesting refinement is the way in which the chimney could be shut away when the grate was out of use. This reduced draughts and obviated the problem of falling soot.

After this transitional stage, the styles were introduced which continued to be popular for the remainder of the century. These comprise, firstly, quite simple and fairly plain types of which those illustrated in Fig. 85 are typical. These show remarkably sparce decoration; the plates over the chimney opening being the most heavily decorated. Many different variations were produced by both Dale and Carron Companies, but the examples illustrated in Fig. 85 show how attached trivets had been added to compensate for the loss of the hob.

The other main type to be produced was highly decorated. Ceramic tiles were added to the splays at the side. The variety of these seems almost endless and they were produced in equal profusion by both Carron and Dale. Figs. 86–87 show typical types although many others could equally have been illustrated. Some Dale examples still retain Gothic Revival and similar tendencies, while Carron produce some very fine canopies. Some examples were even provided with inclusive ash screens which gave a unified appearance to the design.

The use of the tiles is an interesting development for these should reflect heat better than black cast iron. Practicality however, does not appear to have been the driving force; artistic and design factors were paramount. It is difficult to know whether many complaints were received about the black sides which failed to reflect heat. Art Nouveau had arrived and the highly decorated, colourful tiles are now seen to be a part of this movement. According to one's taste, these are considered highly attractive or monstrously ugly— and when employed with a casting having a similar attribute can reach the bottom of the abyss, or the heady heights of magnificence! Likes and dislikes are, however, a matter of personal taste and thus have no relevance here. It is a pity that monochrome photographs fail to do full justice to these bright, decorated tiles and is one very good reason for not illustrating too many. The delights of them are best seen in surviving specimens.

A word of caution to those who become addicts and collect or handle these grates. Firstly, they are very heavy because the casting is large; firebricks are often provided at the back and the tiles cemented in place. Secondly, take care of the tiles, they smash remarkably easily as I have discovered more than once, and this does rather spoil the effect.

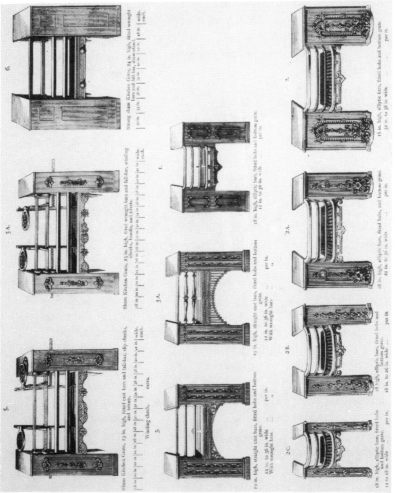

Figs 82–86 Fire grates from the Dale catalogues.

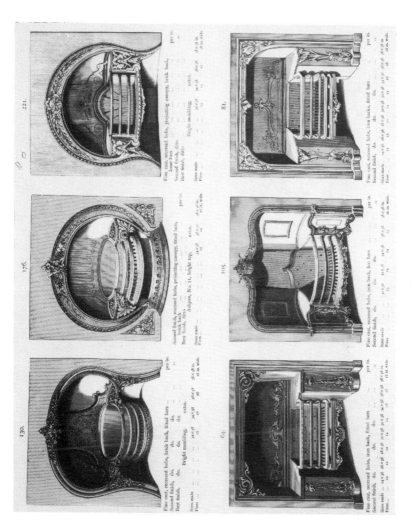

Fig. 83

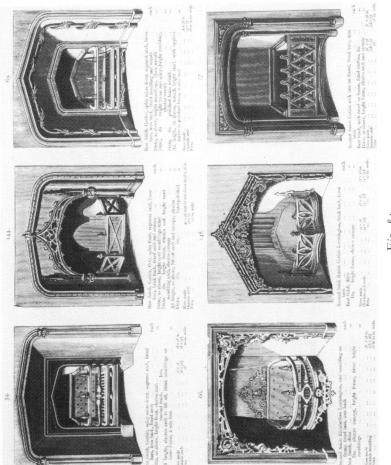

Fig. 84

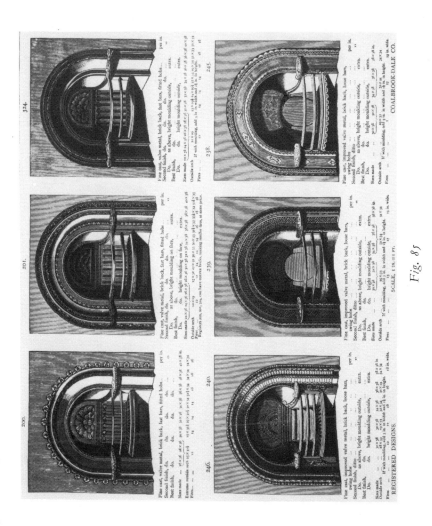

Fig. 85

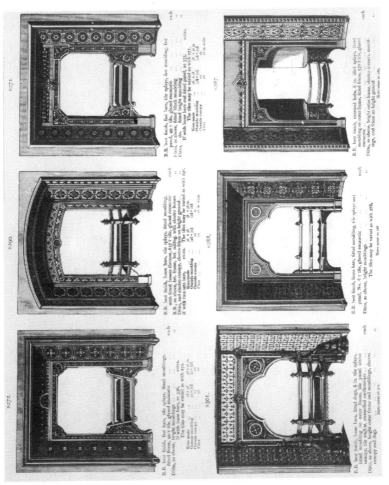

Fig. 86

Fig. 87   Fire grates from the Carron catalogues.

These ideas continued into the early part of the twentieth century, but certainly by the Edwardian period designs had become coarser and less imaginative. It mattered little, for new techniques and ideas were soon, regrettably, to swallow up this earlier, more elegant age.

Before disappearing, the iron casters became very bold and even made complete fireplaces, which included mantelpieces, and sometimes included a large overmantel with mirror. Fireplaces with mantelpieces were more common for smaller, bedroom sized gates. This may be related to weight, a very large drawing room example with overmantle would require a substantial floor to uphold it—and an army of men to erect it!

Fireplaces in the U.S.A.

As with the other articles which have been described, grates do not seem to have crossed to North America, at least not in significant quantities. This dearth of British items in the U.S.A. may have a variety of reasons. One has already been suggested. Antagonism to Britain may have been strong enough to cause a cessation of trade for several decades, but it would be surprising had this not almost vanished in fifty or more years. It must be remembered of course, that the British were not the only colonisers in America and other ideas would arrive from different homelands.

These are surely not the only reasons. Firstly, the U.S.A. was a new, expanding country of which only a small portion had been colonised and conquered. It was unconquered in the sense that the indigenous population had yet to be fully defeated and the country organised by Europeans. The U.S.A. was throughout the nineteenth century, a pioneer country, in which many communities lived as if in a frontier zone. Highways and railways were built to join comparatively scattered pioneer communities. These pioneers, while not necessarily living rough, had a tendency to build in a semi-permanent fashion. Many buildings were of timber, not stone; fireplaces and hearths, like other necessities, were simple; there was no room for frills. Apart from any other consideration, frills were both expensive and, if mass produced, difficult and expensive to transport from industrial centres. There was unlikely to be much money for such fancies when pioneer farms needed all the available capital.

Secondly, there seems, from the American evidence, to be a definite conservative taste. Styles which are known in seventeenth century Britain are retained in America. The simple fireback, cast by traditional methods, locks, ranch style latches, and spur knockers all of wrought iron are typical and fairly frequent examples. The combination of these two reasons fairly effectively rule out the more sophisticated, mass produced British types.

Trivets, Ash Screens and Fenders

Let us now turn our attention to the various accessories of the fireplace.

The disappearance of the hob grate and successors with small, vestigial hobs removed the level surface on which a kettle or saucepan could simmer. A new arrangement was necessary as it was still desirable to keep a kettle in such a position. The result was the production of the *trivet*, which was a small stand hooked onto the firebars. A variety of different designs were produced as is shown by plate 88 from those made by Kenrick. This was undoubtedly a clever idea, for it provided the impetus for modernity while being unsure that the loss of the hob worthwhile. Those who wished to be fashionable were not the only market. It is also necessary to remember the poor unfortunates who had new houses and only the new grates, and thus no choice in the matter. The trivet compensated for the hob quite successfully. Prices were not exceptional; Kenrick were charging eleven shillings (55p) per dozen for a number of the illustrated examples.

While the fronts of grates were made with bars to stop the red hot coals falling out, no guard was provided beneath to stop the spread of the ash or to cover the rather unsightly mess which resulted. The answer to this was provided by

With Bright Tops 2/6 doz extra.

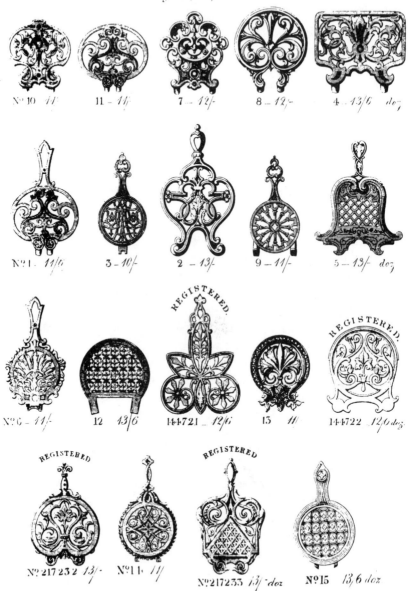

Fig. 88 Trivets from the Kenrick catalogues.

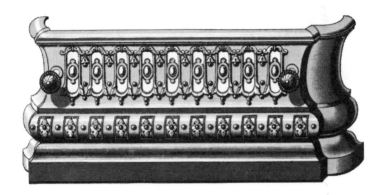

Fig. 89(a)   Ash screens from the Coalbrookdale catalogues.

Fig. 89 (b)   *More ash screens from the Coalbrookdale catalogues.*

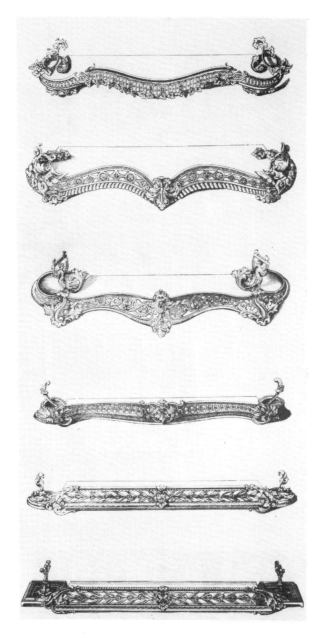

Fig. 90   Fenders from the Coalbrookdale catalogues.

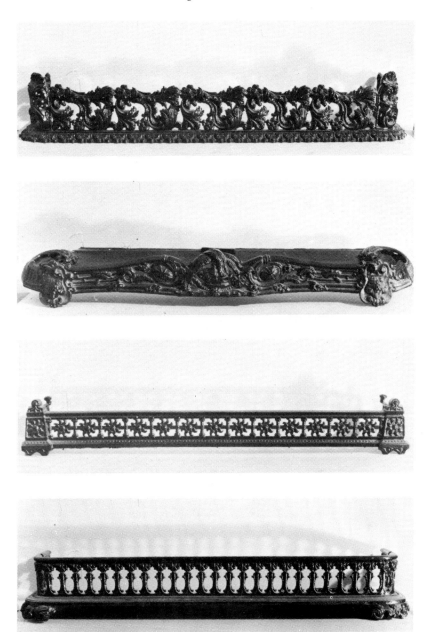

Fig. 91   Fenders now in the Roman Baths Museum collection at Bath.

another interesting invention, that of the *ash screen*. This answered both purposes very well and, in addition, was a decorative feature. On many examples the top is given a type of castellated appearance. Designs varied considerably and even rather fine animals adorned the centre of the piece. A selection produced by the Dale Company can be seem in Fig. 89. It is certain that Carron also produced a considerable variety.

For a long time it had been realised that some form of delineation of the fireplace was necessary, if not essential. Poorer quality coal had the tendency to spit, and smaller, glowing lumps might fall through the bars. A *fender* or curb was an answer as it was some protection against a falling coal from rolling over the carpet and burning a hole—or even worse, of starting a major fire. Fenders were made either with or without attached metal bottoms; obviously those with such an attachment were a better precaution against fires than those without. *Curbs* usually describe those without metal bottoms. Both Carron and Dale produced fenders, and in considerable variety of shape and design. Those illustrated in Fig. 90 from the Dale catalogues are of rectangular designs and splendid curves. Flowers and scroll work in these are particularly pleasant, as also are the figures at either end of No. 135. These designs of considerable quality are probably attributable to the designers which the Dale Company used around the middle of the nineteenth century.

Many other designs were undoubtedly produced. Those illustrated in Fig. 91 reflect the wide variety to be found. The arcading seen in the bottom example and the geometric pattern above are typical, and could belong either to Carron or Dale Companies. The top example is of a fine florid casting and the other is really rather splendid. The centre of this is a crown with a draped fleur-de-lis with oval shields on either side both exhibiting a Union Jack. The inscription beneath reads *Ich Dien*. The ends are of two escutcheons. The whole article is both extremely decorative and a very find piece of casting.

Chapter 6
The Decline of Cast Iron

Since, at the beginning of the volume, space was devoted to the rise, something must be said of the decline of cast iron work.

During the period covered, a great change had taken place in Britain, not only at an industrial, inventive level, but also at a social level. Both pressures have been exerted to different degrees.

To start again with railings; by the end of the first world war social requirements had altered and sanitary arrangements vastly improved. Servants had become less numerous and the conditions in which they lived and worked had markedly improved. The basement and the garret would no longer suffice, nor would the rather dark, damp basement kitchen, which in any event, without the appropriate number of servants, was extremely inconvenient. A meal, hot on leaving the kitchen would be warm when served and cold by the time the rather breathless server had enough composure to eat. Thus the basement and the necessity for an area disappeared—and with it the need for many railings.

From the beginning of the twentieth century, the advent of the semi-detached suburban villas brought new problems. As time progressed these dwelling became ever closer to each other. They had gardens and the owners required defined limits for which cast iron railings might have been expected to provide the answer. This, however, did not happen. If privacy was required from inquisitive next-door neighbours, a wall was much better because it could not be seen through!

Walls were rather expensive, so wooden fences or hedges were tried instead. A hedge gave a softer more rural aspect, but needed time to grow.

These alternatives were fine for the individual but not at all satisfactory for the speculative developer or council builder, whose main concern was cutting costs. Cast iron to him was rather expensive when wire fencing and strands of wire used as a fence were available. Wire strands would be attached to wooden posts at varying intervals and this method of demarkation has only today been modified by the use of more durable, concrete posts. Thus, cast iron as a fencing material was superseded.

Door-furniture seems not to have fared much better. By the end of the first world war, late Victorian designs were declining in popularity. This was one side of the problem. Electricity provided light and power and this power was used to ring a bell when a button was pressed. The electric bell had a great advantage; it was loud and could be installed in the most useful place and when ringing, would be unlikely to go unnoticed. This replaced the door knocker. Smart, plain, new chromium plated steel was now used for the letter-plate. It only required a rub to look very bright and clean. Thus departed the old letter-plate. Could the fine door knob survive? No, these too departed; the designs were too flamboyant. But perhaps this is not the whole story. The introduction of various types of patent locks with small keys caused the final decline. This type of lock closes with comparative ease and does not need a mighty tug.

Scrapers, as has been hinted at, also went the same way. Certainly the coconut mat and other fibre mat producers had a field day; but there was also the metal wire mat, which had a chain effect, and other derivatives of this type.

The disappearance of the door-porter is less understandable; rising hinges became less prevalent, but the problem of wind never vanishes. Perhaps here it is mainly the change in artistic fashion; the types still produced were of Victorian design, which was too flamboyant.

As we have seen, the fireplace has been a constantly evolving feature, castings diminishing as a result of further evolution and changes in fashion. The growing habit of the building trade to complete items before placing them within a building began during the early part of the twentieth century. Whole fireplaces were provided as complete assembled articles and which included tiled, fendered hearths. This made the fireplace opening even smaller, but increased the chimney piece as a central, focal point by contrasting the material used in it with that of the plastered wall. This use of contrasting wall and chimney piece material was an attempt to replace the loss of plaster and other details which gave feature to a room. This was undoubtedly a sharp blow to the cast iron grate producers, but it was not the only force at work. Methods were being devised to reduce the quantity of draught in the grate, and the amount of fuel consumed. The small, tight-fitting grates inserted within these new chimney pieces had ash screens provided with opening and closing ventilator holes. These removed the need for the old ash screen. These grates were more efficient and provided a controllable draught which kept a fire burning within a chimney piece which did not smoke. No wonder the builders used these new types.

The power of gas and electricity provided fires which required no tending and stoking, and so in a number of places, coal fires vanished altogether. In more recent years, central heating has had an even more drastic effect on the future of the coal fire. Today, central heating is often provided as a standard fitting in many new houses. This is a very good illustration of the way in which history is a living, continuous process.

Lack of enthusiasm for the design of the later Victorian period undoubtedly had some effect, but it was almost certainly less persuasive than the improvements provided by the new developments.

The demise of the domestic cast iron industry is thus complete. Other materials, improved types, totally new ideas, changes of fashion and social conditions have all been contributing factors. A new age has arrived which, in turn, will pass and be succeeded by another era, the materials of which only our children and grandchildren will know.

Chapter 7
Collecting

While nothing will be said of the monetary value of these items, as prices fluctuate, it is perhaps pertinent to say something about the value of preserving or collecting these items. What follows is true of all the varying items discussed within this book.

Since the second world war, the whole of Britain has witnessed a massive increase in demolition of slums, properties said to be sub-standard, and of buildings still with plenty of life remaining, but merely making space for redevelopment. This is particularly the case in city centres. A discussion of the merits, or otherwise, of this wholesale destruction does not belong in this book. The important thing to remember, however, is that demolition is happening and happening fast; and is likely to continue for the rest of the century.

This provides a massive challenge to those interested in any aspect of the past, however recent. This great period of demolition will undoubtedly put masses of every conceivable type of domestic attatchment under the scrutiny of the demolition contractor—and his hammer.

Should the opportunity to collect the material be missed, then details of a great period of domestic history will be rather scarce. Inevitably, through inability to collect or even, remove items, much will be lost.

The very importance of all this material is then to be found in the realisation that this is one aspect of one hundred and fifty years of social and domestic history; at a time when social and technological changes were accelerating.

Renovation

Whatever the style and wherever the the items exist, they are always worth looking after.

Should the reader wish to renovate his balconies and railings, he has a considerable amount of work ahead. Tapping with a hammer will remove much of the paint, and a dental probe will remove the remainder from the crevices. Lead rosettes should be burnished with a wire brush and then the whole item re-painted, probably starting with an anti-rust primer—leaving aside, of course, the lead rosettes.

If collectors wish to improve the appearance of their door furniture, there are no short cuts. Paint stripper is a waste of time as too many different types of paint usually cover the design. The best method is lightly to tap away the worst deposits of paint with a small hammer—but, remember, cast iron can be brittle and if hit too forcibly, may break. The remainder should be dug out with the equivalent of an old dental probe. The design can then be painted, possibly using an anti-rust primer before the top coat is applied.

Grates and fireplace accessories would originally have been black-leaded. How best to treat the article will depend upon its new use. If in a house centrally heated, or one not using coal fires, the best method is to clean and then paint with plastic emulsion paint, possibly adding an anti-rust primer if in a bad condition. However, should, again, the intention be to use the grate for its original purpose, black leading, which is tedious but rewarding, is the only answer.

This treatment also applies equally to the accessory items, usage being the determining factor. Whichever method is ultimately used, the result will be surprisingly pleasant. Fenders should, if being used for purely decorative purposes, be gloss rather than matt finished as the appearance will be enhanced.

The U.S.A.

One place where domestic cast iron of British origin might be expected is in the U.S.A. and other countries where there has been British influence and settlement.

Yet strangely enough, this appears not to be so in the U.S.A. The American War of Independence may well have given Anglo-American trade a knock. But I think the trade in domestic items was already waning during the eighteenth century, if the evidence of shop loads of pottery leaving Barnstaple in Devon for the U.S.A. is any guide. Trade accelerated until around 1700 and then showed a steady decline during the eighteenth century. It may be that worsening relations with Britain failed to encourage any renewed traffic or continuation of the old.

The other thing to be remembered is that the amount of the American Continent colonised by 1830 was still quite small, and not only by people of British origin.

All material illustrated shows that the iron work produced in the States at this time shows little or no affinity to its British counterparts. A far greater proportion of American material is still wrought iron, whereas in Britain by 1770–1780, iron foundries were quite well established.

In the U.S.A., traditional methods of casting were employed and certainly some work was of the same type which was general use in Britain in the seventeenth century, particularly firebrick types. There were, however, no true iron foundries for casting in Pennsylvania before 1820.

By this time the American taste, although influenced by Europe, was developing in its own direction. That taste seemed to spurn cast iron for decorative purposes if Henry C. Mercer is correct, for he asserts in *The Bible is Iron*, that its use had ceased by 1830 or at the latest by 1840.

Thus it seems that British examples of cast iron which are now to be found in the U.S.A. are imports. But they are not consignments from shippers or producers, but probably from much more recent travellers from the U.S.A. to Britain who then returned with items which took their fancy.

Index